A Manager's Guide to PR Projects

A Manager's Guide to PR Projects, Second Edition picks up where classic public relations textbooks leave off. It provides hands-on guidance in planning the preliminary research for a public relations project and creating a plan to achieve specific goals, guiding the reader through managing the project's implementation. It contains worksheets that can be used for a visual representation of the planning process for both student edification and presentation to clients. The book is designed as a user-friendly guide to take the reader through the four-step public relations planning process from a number of vantage points. Intended as a learning tool for use in both the class and beyond, this book's approaches are based on real experiences in the management of communications projects designed to meet organizational goals through achieving public relations objectives.

This fully revised second edition offers PR students and practitioners new material that includes the following:

- The impact of social media on each phase of the planning process.

- Digital approaches to strategic and summative research, message dissemination and public engagement.

- Strategies to enhance accountability.

- Ethics considerations in the planning process.

- Updated print and web-based resources for PR managers.

Patricia J. Parsons spent 26 years as a Professor of Public Relations in the Department of Communication Studies at Mount Saint Vincent University in Halifax, Canada after a career in health communication and writing. She is the author of a dozen books including *Ethics in Public Relations: A Guide to Best Practice* and *Beyond Persuasion: Communication Strategies for Healthcare Managers in the Digital Age*.

A Manager's Guide to PR Projects

A Practical Approach

Second Edition

Patricia J. Parsons

Routledge
Taylor & Francis Group

NEW YORK AND LONDON

Second edition published 2018
by Routledge
711 Third Avenue, New York, NY 10017

and by Routledge
2 Park Square, Milton Park, Abingdon, Oxon OX14 4RN

Routledge is an imprint of the Taylor & Francis Group, an informa business

First edition published by Routledge 2003

Library of Congress Cataloging in Publication Data
Names: Parsons, Patricia (Patricia Houlihan), author.
Title: A manager's guide to PR projects : a practical approach /
Patricia J. Parsons.
Description: Second edition. | New York : Routledge, 2018.
Identifiers: LCCN 2017027520| ISBN 9781138099920 (hardback) |
ISBN 9781138099937 (pbk.)
Subjects: LCSH: Public relations—Management.
Classification: LCC HD59 .P355 2018 | DDC 659.2—dc23
LC record available at https://lccn.loc.gov/2017027520

ISBN: 978-1-138-09992-0 (hbk)
ISBN: 978-1-138-09993-7 (pbk)
ISBN: 978-1-315-10385-3 (ebk)

Typeset in Bembo and Stone Sans
by Florence Production Ltd, Stoodleigh, Devon, UK

Contents

Figures

Before we Begin

PREFACE TO THE SECOND EDITION

When the first edition of *A Manager's Guide to PR Projects: A Practical Approach* was published in 2003 the world of public relations and corporate communication was a much simpler place. Given that social media platforms were in their infancy, public relations managers could be assured that a meticulously researched, well-crafted, strategic communication/public relations plan would generally hit its marks, achieving most if not all its objectives with little unanticipated interference. Over the course of the intervening years all of that has changed. In addition, the world in a broader sense is a different place. What has not changed, however, is the fundamental need for public relations and communications practitioners to understand the basic concepts of planning, and to embrace these fundamentals as a framework for approaching all situations.

Just as with the first edition, this new edition picks up where classic public relations planning textbooks leave off. It provides practical, hands-on guidance in planning the preliminary research for a public relations project and creating a plan to achieve specific goals, guiding the reader through important aspects of managing the project's implementation and finally evaluating the results. Unlike other planning textbooks, this is a workbook in the truest sense of the word. It contains valuable worksheets that can be used for visual representation of the planning process for both student learning and for presentation to clients. It is written and designed to maximize the students' or practitioners' engagement with the material.

This is an easy book to read; however, its usefulness to both students and practitioners is in its clear focus on guiding the reader through the planning process while developing the fundamental paradigm necessary for more complex strategic planning in the future. This book is a tool: a practical approach.

Much of the overall planning paradigm has not changed since the publication of the first edition. What has changed is how that planning thought process is operationalized.

Since the publication of the first edition, communication technology has become significantly more advanced, not to mention ubiquitous, with the fine-tuning of a variety of digital tools. Since the world of public relations relies largely on communication tools and tactics, this workbook has been updated to include additional material on the digital tools available for strategic and summative research, for message dissemination and for public engagement. In addition, concerns about the ethics of organizational activities have multiplied alongside unremitting, external public scrutiny since the first edition was first published. Considering the ethics of one's creative strategies is essential prior to implementation. This aspect of planning has been included in this edition to reflect the changing focus on ethics in practice.

One caveat: since this book does provide a variety of templates to assist in the planning and implementation of public relations projects, it may be easy for the reader to begin to believe that this is the only approach—that the templates are to be followed unfailingly. This is not the case. The reader needs to be aware that there are many ways to approach the planning process. What is contained in this book is based on my thirty-plus years of developing client plans and supervising hundreds of client-based student plans. It is what I recommend to beginning practitioners, as well as practitioners who need to be reminded from time to time of the fundamentals. As your experience and judgment develop, individualized, creative approaches to specific client issues will become apparent. I propose that you use this workbook as a starting point from which to develop a proactive, ethical planning philosophy for public relations and corporate communication.

Please let me know how you have been able to use this book.

Patricia J. Parsons APR, FCPRS
Twitter: @pparsons07
professorparsons.com

CHAPTER 1

PR Project Planning in the Twenty-first Century

VOCABULARY

By the end of this chapter, you should be able to define and discuss the following:

- public relations
- public relations process
- project planning
- systems
- subsystem
- input

- throughput
- output
- management
- integrity
- ethics

DEFINING PUBLIC RELATIONS

Public relations, as a field of practice, has been defined in many ways by many writers and public relations practitioners over the years. How you define public relations depends on a number of factors including the following:

- your specific educational background in the field (for example: journalism, English, marketing, public relations);

- your level of education in PR or related fields (for example: certificate, bachelor's degree, master's degree);

- the books, magazines, and journals you have read (for example public relations textbooks versus marketing textbooks);

- the professional associations to which you belong (for example: the International Association of Business Communicators, the Public Relations Society of America, the Public Relations Students' Society of America, the American Academy of Advertising, the Canadian Public Relations Society, the Chartered Institute of Public Relations UK) or on the other hand, to which you do not belong;

- your experience in public relations and its related communication fields (for example: advertising, marketing, graphic design).

For you as an individual practitioner, these are some of the factors that provide you with a picture of precisely what public relations is and has been through history. However, much has changed in the world of communication-related fields over the past decade. In spite of these massive changes, specifically in communication technology, there are fundamental aspects of how we define public relations that have not changed. Let's examine some of the formal definitions of public relations offered by our professional associations.

The Public Relation Society of America says that: "At its core, public relations is about influencing, engaging and building a relationship with key stakeholders to contribute to the way an organization is perceived" (www.prsa.org/about/about-pr/all-about-pr/). In this definition it is clear that the concepts of *influence*, *engagement*, and *relationships* continue to underpin both PR's responsibilities and the value it adds to its organizations.

The Canadian Public Relations Society (CPRS) defines public relations as follows: "Public relations is the strategic management of relationships between an organization and its diverse publics, through the use of communication, to achieve mutual understanding, realize organizational goals and serve the public interest" (www.cprs.ca/aboutus/mission.aspx).

CPRS also goes on to describe that strategic public relations practice is *managed* and *accountable*, *aligned* with the overall goals of the organization, *intentional* and *deliberate*, and *measurable* and *relevant*. This concept of public relations as a *strategic* function suggests that public relations activities must be purposeful, intentional, and above all, **planned**.

The Chartered Institute of Public Relations (CIPR UK) in the UK frames the practice slightly differently in their focus on reputation management. CIPR (UK) defines public relations as follows:

> Public Relations is about reputation—the result of what you do, what you say and what others say about you . . . Public Relations is the discipline which looks after reputation, with the aim of earning understanding and support and influencing opinion and behaviour [sic]. It is the planned and sustained effort to establish and maintain goodwill and mutual understanding between an organisation [sic] and its publics . . .
>
> (www.cipr.co.uk/content/careers-advice/what-pr)

In spite of CIPR (UK)'s frame of reputation, you can see clearly that there is still an emphasis on influence and planning.

So, although these may at first glance appear to be differing perspectives on what public relations actually is, there are more commonalities than there are differences. This book is based on a number of commonly held beliefs about the practice of public relations:

- Public relations is a management function that assists the organization to reach its goals.

- Public relations is a strategic process of research, planning, implementation, and evaluation.

- Engagement and influence are two of the key components of the objectives of the PR/communication planning process.

- Public relations utilizes a variety of targeted communications tools and techniques to help organizations develop and maintain mutually beneficial relationships with publics of importance to them in reaching their goals.

- Public relations practice requires both managerial and technical skills, creativity, flexibility, and above all integrity.

These beliefs guide the management of public relations projects.

DEFINING MANAGEMENT

As a public relations manager, you will be required to be more than a technician. You will be required to do more than create content, monitor social media channels, and organize media conferences. You will be responsible for seeing the bigger picture.

Management as a term is a bit like the term "public relations": there are as many definitions as there are managers. Most definitions again, however, have some commonalities. The following are some of those common factors:

- Management is a process of getting things done efficiently and effectively.

- Management accomplishes its goals through and with people and the strategic use of other organizational resources, including time and money.

- There are four fundamental activities that managers use to accomplish their goals. These are planning, organizing, leading, and controlling.

It's worth noting that these sound a lot like the activities we will identify as part of the four-step public relations process—and they are. Thus, for our purposes, ***the public relations process itself is our fundamental management tool.***

Whereas small organizations may have only one main manager, larger organizations—whether they are for-profit, not-for-profit, or government ventures—usually have a number of managers. A public relations manager may have a department of one to manage, or a department of many. Every project, however, whether carried out by one person or many, must be planned and managed for it to achieve its goals.

Here is the working definition of public relations that guides the process presented in this book:

MODERN PUBLIC RELATIONS **is a management function that uses a process of research, planning, implementation, and evaluation to help an organization achieve its communication and relationship goals**

DEFINING A "PROJECT"

This book is titled *A Manager's Guide to PR Projects*. Clearly we need a working definition of the term *project* as we are using it in this context. The Oxford online dictionary defines a project as ". . . an individual or collaborative enterprise that is carefully planned to achieve a particular aim . . ." (https://en.oxforddictionaries.com/definition/project). If we use this definition, a public relations project can be anything from the development of a simple media release (which begins as an idea in someone's mind, is researched, outlined, written, and, at some point, evaluated) up to the most complex strategies for solving organizational problems that stem from external and/or internal relationships. In other words, an excellent public relations practitioner will use a project planning thought process for everything from the largest to the smallest project, rather than flying by the seat of his or her pants. Even a tweet needs to be planned. We have ample anecdotal evidence to understand that we use unplanned tweets at our peril.

As you become more experienced, you will begin to realize that you have internalized this process, and simple projects often no longer require a formal, written plan. Sometimes, however, seemingly simple challenges can stump you; when this happens you can revert to this useful exercise whenever you need it. More complex strategies always require a written plan using the four-step process, modified and adapted to the situation at a particular point in the organization's history. This workbook is designed for use in strategic communication planning to achieve public relations objectives.

PUBLIC RELATIONS PROCESS: A SYSTEMS EXPLANATION

Systems theory provides a useful paradigm for examining the relationships between an organization and its publics, and for understanding and applying public relations process.

If we consider the notion that an organization exists within an environment that exerts economic, social, political, and technological pressures on it, we can see that the publics with which that organization interacts are also part of that environment. As such, these publics (whose boundaries the organization defines) are both subject to these same pressures *and* capable of being part of the pressures exerted on the organization.

Both the organization and its publics are interacting units of the system and are subject to environmental pressures. These twenty-first century pressures are as follows:

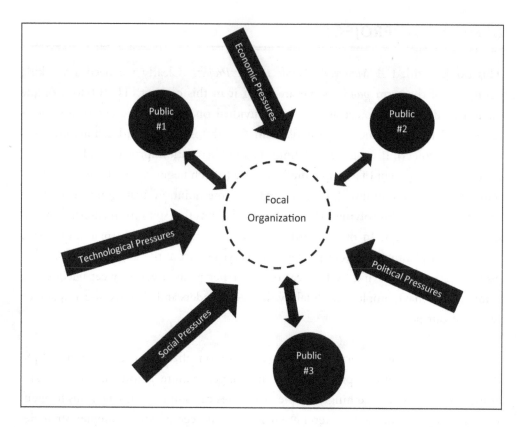

FIGURE 1.1 The Organization as a System

- **P**olitical

- **E**conomic

- **S**ocial

- **T**echnological

The identification of these four aspects of an organization's environment have given rise to what is now referred to as a PEST analysis. (We'll come back to this in Chapter 2.)

Also, note that the arrows from the organization are two-headed, indicating that interaction (communication), in the ideal model, is two-way. This entire workbook assumes that excellent public relations is based on a two-way communication model.

When an organization feels pressures from outside its boundaries (and sometimes from inside those same boundaries) it can choose either to maintain the *status quo* or to adapt to the pressures. Maintaining the *status quo* usually results in an organization that is unable to progress and flourish. Adaptation, on the other hand, allows the organization to identify and solve its problems and to capitalize on opportunities (see Chapter 2 for more specific definitions of these terms).

If we take a closer look at the focal organization, we can see another system. This system comprises the interacting units that make up the organization itself. The public relations function is one of those units, and it is within this subsystem that the public relations process is carried out. In systems terms, within the public relations function itself, *input* consists of pressures, data, communication from internal or external publics, activities of publics that bring pressure to bear on the organization, and so on. *Throughput* is the public relations process itself (carrying out research, planning, implementing plans, and evaluating plans), and *output* comprises the messages (and how they are carried) to various publics, both internal and external (examples of output include tweets, blogs, videos, events, publicity). Keep in mind that the term "messages" in public relations can mean messages in the overt, literal sense as illustrated by the foregoing examples, but they can also be more implied. For example, it is not just the specific communication activities that make up the organization's output in the public relations process, but its actions as well. In addition, the development or adaptation of policies in response to feedback from important publics can be significant public relations approaches whose messages may appear more subliminal, but are just as key to the development of strong relationships with publics. Thus, two-way communication and the adaptation of the organization to its publics and its environment also constitute outputs.

These four steps—research, plan, implement, and evaluate—form the basis for what we call public relations process (see Figure 1.2).

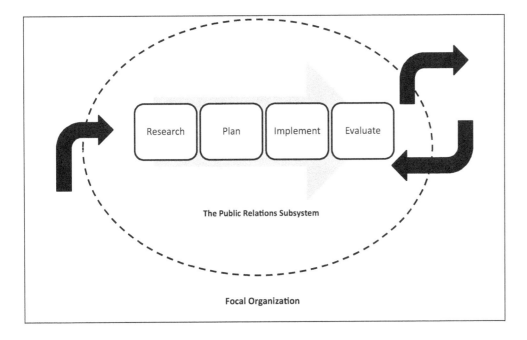

FIGURE 1.2 Public Relations as an Organizational Subsystem

UPDATING THE PR PROCESS FOR THE TWENTY-FIRST CENTURY

By now you should have figured out that this so-called **public relations process** as we have come to know it, is really nothing more or less than a systematic way to make well-founded, strategic decisions. Furthermore, it is not unique to the field of public relations *per se*. For example, a medical doctor uses a similar process when he or she gathers both subjective and objective information about a patient's condition, determines a diagnosis, decides on a treatment plan, then follows up to determine the outcome, changing the approach, if necessary, based on that outcome. Using that process to deal with the communications issues within an organization is, however, the purview of the public relations profession.

Back in 1963 a public relations expert named John Marston wrote a book titled *The Nature of Public Relations*. Ahead of his time in many ways, Marston was one of the first practitioners to suggest that public relations is more than a seat-of-the-pants activity: the best public relations programs and projects are planned. Further, he was the first to articulate a simple, four-step process for the systematic and strategic development of these plans. He offered what has become almost legendary in PR circles: the RACE formula.

Here is what he meant:

- **R**: Research—Marston was clear about the need for research as the first step in the PR process.

- **A**: Action—Marston suggested that the next step would comprise planning the action.

- **C**: Communicate—In the RACE formula, this term "communicate" refers to the process by which the public relations activity is implemented.

- **E**: Evaluate—Marston's final step indicated the need for evaluation of the outcomes of the activities—and he was one of the first to do so.

The twenty-first century requires us to be very clear about our meanings and choose our words carefully so that we can be understood. For this reason, Marston's handy acronym, as appealing as it might be, clearly does not really say precisely what it means. These days we still use his conceptual approach to planning, but it's imperative that we be clearer when we delineate the four steps. For that reason, we refer to them not as research, action, communication, and evaluation. Rather we clearly label them as research, plan, implement, and evaluate. That way there is no confusion about what happens in each step. But we thank John Marston for his early contribution.

Let's examine each step a bit more carefully.

Research:

During the research phase, the public relations practitioner gathers information from a variety of sources. These could include such secondary sources as organizational records, governmental statistics, textbooks, or journals. Often, data gathering also includes such primary methods as surveys, interviews, and focus groups. (See Chapter 2 for further explanation of primary and secondary sources and methods.)

The communication or public relations audit, which includes both primary and secondary sources for information, is a formalized method of assessing the communication activities of an organization and thus is also a research tool.

Also included in the research phase is analysis. It is not enough simply to gather the information, it must be analyzed so that the problem or opportunity may be identified (see more about problems and opportunities in Chapter 2).

Plan:

The most important aspect of the planning stage is setting objectives for the plan. These are the desired outcomes. In simple terms, you have to know where you want to go. Once the objectives are developed, it becomes feasible to look at message development, select channels and vehicles, and determine how, when, and by whom the plan will be implemented.

Implement:

During the implementation phase, the plan is carried out. When developing a strategy in the first place, however, the strategist needs to deal with managing the implementation. For example, how resources will be utilized for execution of the plan is an important part of examining the implementation prior to actually putting the plan into action.

Evaluate:

The final phase is evaluation. The strategist always plans how the project will be evaluated while preparing the initial plan. The evaluation phase itself is really ongoing, although it appears to be the last phase. Evaluation strategies are always developed in direct response to the objectives set for each specific public, and the measurement of outcomes is used as research data for future strategies thus making this a feedback loop and a circular rather than linear process.

ETHICS AND INTEGRITY IN PR PLANNING

Earlier in this chapter when we summarized the definitions of public relations and enumerated the commonalities of the definitions, the final belief about public relations indicated that in addition to creativity and technical skill, public relations must be practiced with *integrity*. In fact, ethical considerations should be a part of every PR plan you create, from the smallest (for example: Is this tweet we're planning really appropriate? Will it harm anyone?) to the largest (for example: Will our decision to withhold information on potential hazards built into one of our products affect anyone adversely?). Let's begin by defining integrity.

C.S. Lewis suggested a definition that is my personal favorite: *Integrity means doing the right thing even when no one is looking.*

This definition suggests first that if you are a person of integrity, you know what that "right" thing is. Second, it suggests that a person of integrity does that "right" thing not simply for selfish reasons. In other words, that person would do the "right" thing even if there were no threat of punishment and no potential for personal reward. That action would be undertaken because the person of integrity realizes that doing the "right" thing is simply the way to behave. The problem, of course, is that always knowing the "right" thing to do is not as simple as it sounds. That's why there are guides to ethical decision-making that public relations practitioners can refer to when faced with evaluating the ethics of their PR plans.

Based on fundamental aspects of ethics in general, The Pillars of PR Ethics are a useful guide for that kind of decision-making (see Figure 1.3).

Pillars of Public Relations Ethics

- Non-maleficence (do no harm)
- Beneficience (do good)
- Truth-telling (honesty)
- Confidentiality (privacy)
- Justice (fairness and social responsibility)

FIGURE 1.3 The Pillars of Public Relations Ethics

Adapted from Parsons, P. (2016) *Ethics in public relations: A guide to best practice.* 3rd ed. London: Kogan Page.

These pillars are based on the following ethical considerations that are fundamental to making decisions that are at the very least ethically defensible:

- Above all, we should make every effort to do no harm in our public relations activities.

- Whenever possible, we should look for opportunities to proactively do something good.

- All of our activities must be honest, transparent, and never seek to mislead.

- Our activities should not breach confidentiality or personal privacy.

- Decisions that we make should be as fair and equitable as we can make them.

Ethics considerations need to be an integral part of every plan and every activity undertaken by PR practitioners. At the end of this chapter you will find an **ETHICS CHECKLIST** that you should have by your side whenever you are engaged in planning public relations and communications projects. Eventually, it will become second nature to you to consider these PR Pillars in every decision you make as a practicing professional.

USING THIS BOOK

This book is designed as a user-friendly guide that will introduce you to basic components of the planning process so that you will see it as a way of thinking that will become your paradigm for increasingly complex situations in which you will find yourself over the course of a public relations career.

It leads you through the four-step public relations planning process from any one of a number of vantage points. You may be a manager, a public relations student, a PR practitioner who needs a review, a marketing specialist who needs to understand PR thinking, or someone outside the field who has an interest in public relations planning. Each of you will find something useful and practical in the pages that follow. It is not intended as a crutch, rather as a learning tool for use both in class and beyond. Its approaches are based on real experiences in the management of public relations and communications projects designed to meet organizational goals through achieving public relations objectives.

The worksheets at the end of each chapter are designed to be copied for your personal use as you work through the planning process; some are even useful as documents that might be shared with a client or employer as supplementary material in a final written plan.

This workbook presupposes that you are reading, or have read, a variety of complementary materials that explain in greater detail some of the terms used. There is a vocabulary list at the beginning of each chapter. These are terms that are used in the text that follows, but that beg fuller explanation toward which the resource list for each chapter will lead you.

Onward!

Now that we have examined the purpose of this workbook and set our framework for discussing the management of public relations projects, we'll begin the real work of strategic public relations—creating the strategy.

The remainder of this workbook is devoted to the four phases of the public relations process. Each section begins with a listing of important terminology (which you should look up in several theory books if you are unfamiliar with any of them), provides brief background on the step of the process, and then moves quickly to tools that you can use to work through the strategic process.

This is where the creative fun of professional public relations really lies!

Ethics Checklist

Considering the ethical implications of PR activities is integral to the planning process. Before determining overall strategy, and before implementing any of the planned tactics, complete this worksheet to evaluate the ethical implications, if any.

PART 1: DURING THE PLANNING PROCESS

☐ We have identified the affected public(s).

☐ The plan will not cause any of the identified publics harm, or perceived potential harm has been minimized.

☐ The plan will not deceive or mislead in any way.

☐ We have not missed an opportunity to proactively do "good" for our public(s).

☐ The plan does not breach confidentiality of any affected parties.

☐ The plan treats all affected parties fairly.

☐ We have balanced our loyalties to public(s), employer/client and society.

☐ The plan "feels" right.

PART 2: AFTER THE STRATEGY/TACTIC IS DESIGNED

☐ If challenged about the ethics of the plan, we are able to provide a salient, ethics-based defense of the approaches.

☐ The plan still feels "right."

☐ We would still feel "good" about the plan if we were the affected public.

☐ We would feel comfortable about transparently publicizing our approach via traditional or social media.

CHAPTER 2

The Research Phase

VOCABULARY

By the end of this chapter, you should be able to define and discuss the following:

- applied research
- theoretical research
- primary research
- secondary research
- primary sources
- secondary sources
- survey

- focus group
- public relations/ communication audit
- metrics
- analysis
- public relations problem
- public relations opportunity

DATA-GATHERING: AN EVERYDAY PROCESS

Let's presume for a moment that you are sitting at your desk reading this chapter. It's three o'clock in the afternoon and you've already had a very busy day. When you got out of bed this morning, you had to get dressed. Look down at what you're wearing right now.

Have you changed your clothes since this morning? If you did, why did you change? Presume for a moment that you are still wearing the same clothes you dressed in when you got up. How did you decide what you would wear today? Getting dressed is an activity that all of us do every day, but we don't usually wear the same clothes (even people who wear uniforms usually have the odd day off from it). How, then, did you decide on the clothes that you now see on yourself?

If you're like most of us, however unconsciously, you gathered a host of data, analyzed it, then made a decision. Eventually, you will evaluate that decision, but let's stick to the data-gathering for a moment more. Here are some of the pieces of data you might have considered before you got dressed:

- What is the weather like?

- What clothes are clean?

- What do I have to do today?

- Who am I likely to see today?

- What kind of impression do I want to make?

- How do I feel today?

Some of the methods you might use to gather answers to these questions are the following:

- checking your weather app on your phone;

- looking out the window;

- observing the floor and/or the closet;

- checking your online calendar;

- asking a significant other for an opinion.

You will analyze all this information, use it to figure out your goal (e.g. to be comfortable, to get that new job, to impress someone special), and then you will create a plan of action. And it's likely that your plan of action will be flawed if you don't gather and analyze this data, resulting in outcomes that you may not like.

You may not be aware of it, but your actions to collect data and analyze it constitute research. So, for our purposes in managing the public relations process, we will use the following definition:

> RESEARCH **is a deliberate, planned, and organized process for collection and analysis of data for the purpose of determining an organization's public relations problems, opportunities, and possible solutions.**

WHAT RESEARCH CAN ACCOMPLISH

Let's go back for a moment to your morning decision-making process about your daily wardrobe. Consider this scenario: for several weeks, you have been preparing for a very important job interview that is scheduled for early this morning. You wake up late and giving little thought to what you'll be wearing, you throw on the first thing you see. You arrive at the interview on time, but the receptionist takes one look at you and figures that you must be in the wrong place. You are wearing a rumpled shirt and jacket and you are soaking wet. You hadn't realized that it was raining until it was too late. You have failed to do appropriate and sufficient research, thereby decreasing the likelihood that you will achieve your ultimate goal. And the key to understanding this process is being acutely aware that data-gathering at the outset—research in other words—is essential to goal achievement.

Conducting research before embarking on any kind of public relations venture is critical to its success. For example, before you launch a new employee online newsletter to keep them informed, you need to find out what employees need and want to know, but you also need to determine what employees believe is the most effective and credible way to receive information, and their online reading habits. If you fail to collect and use this information, you may find yourself with a shiny new newsletter that no one reads, resulting in your inability to achieve your goals; in the end, this costs your organization or client money.

On a larger scale, research is central to the strategic planning process so that you can answer the following overarching questions:

- Where are we now?

- Where do we want to go?

- What is likely to be the best route to get there?

Organizations have saved themselves thousands of dollars by conducting research before launching communication campaigns or determining the best way to deal with feedback from publics. For example, what would be the point of trying to change a perceived negative image about your organization until you know the real perceptions held by your publics?

The bottom line on research is that it affects the bottom line, whatever your organization's bottom line might be. In the long run it can save you money, time, resources, and effort.

Research can accomplish many things. The following are some of the key things it can accomplish for public relations. Research can:

1. Provide essential information about the environment (social, economic, political, and technological) that has or has had an impact on the organization and its publics.

2. Identify and describe the PR problems and/or opportunities that exist.

3. Determine the type and size of the public relations effort required.

4. Determine the extent to which there is a need for this approach.

5. Target your specific public(s).

6. Describe the specific characteristics of your public(s).

7. Describe the health of your organization/client's relationships with specific publics.

8. Assist in the articulation of your message(s).

9. Identify appropriate and potentially effective vehicles, tactics, and channels to reach specific publics.

10. Identify the best metrics to use to measure the eventual outcomes from your PR effort.

11. Enhance the credibility of the public relations function with top management by contributing to the bottom line—whatever that might be (for example, if you work in a corporate entity, profits would be the bottom line.

If you work in health promotion, changes in the targeted behavior will be the bottom line.)

Regardless of the kind of business within which you work (or will work someday), you will be expected to provide data to support what is referred to as *evidence-based* decisions. Simply put, you need to have solid evidence to provide a rationale for what you do, why you are doing it, when you are doing it and for whom it will be done. The only way to be able to do all of this is to conduct research before you begin.

PROBLEM OR OPPORTUNITY?

Being able to recognize a *problem* or *opportunity* and to define it succinctly is one of the most important outcomes of the data analysis portion of the research phase, and no research is complete without it. The following are useful definitions that will help both you and your client/employer to understand the planning process that will follow:

> **A PUBLIC RELATIONS PROBLEM is a relationship or communication issue that has been identified as a result of past events, current activities, and future projections, and which is likely to impede the organization from reaching its goals.**

Thus a problem emanates directly from weaknesses in the relationships that an organization has with one or more publics. A problem may be, for example, a public's lack of *information* about the organization, its policies, its products or services, or issues it represents. It may also be an *attitude* or perception issue: one or more publics may hold negative perceptions about the organization or what it represents. This negative attitude may or may not have resulted (yet) in the public taking action on that attitude. This, of course, leads naturally to the final kind of problem, *actions* that a public has taken as a result of its unhealthy relationship with the organization. These actions might be picketing outside your offices, posting negative comments online, boycotting your products, etc. When determining an organization's public relations problems, a PR practitioner must consider all of these domains: information, attitude and action.

An opportunity offers a different perspective, and is equally important:

> **A** PUBLIC RELATIONS OPPORTUNITY **is the identification of a juncture of events and objectives that provides an optimal window for using communication strategies to enhance an organization's internal and/or external relationships and thus further the organization's goals.**

An opportunity emerges from an analysis of the organization's strengths in its relationships and communications activities with its publics (what's working well) and its responses to its environment. In addition, strengths may be identified within the organization itself. For example, the appointment of a new CEO with a fundamental understanding of the value of public relations as a management function may present a number of opportunities to strengthen relationships and PR processes within the organization.

HOW RESEARCH IS DONE

Research textbooks discuss two major categories of research:

- First, **academic research** is conducted, usually by scholars, in an effort to add to the general body of knowledge in a particular discipline. The practical applications may not be immediately apparent. For example, a public relations professor might research public relations ethics to explain how and why PR practitioners do what they do. Then he or she might develop a theory to explain the ethical decision-making process. Eventually this theory might contribute to the development of an ethical decision-making framework that you, the practitioner, could actually use on a day-to-day basis.

- **Applied research**, on the other hand, is research that is conducted within a professional field. Both scholars and practitioners might be engaged in applied research, but usually for different reasons. In the process of planning and managing public relations strategies and campaigns, public relations practitioners are engaged in applied research.

In terms of techniques that public relations practitioners might use to gather data during the research phase of developing the PR plan, there are two general categories that we need to differentiate between.

Secondary research is the term used to describe the process of collecting information from sources where the original data have been accumulated already. In this situation you are not actually collecting the data yourself. When conducting this secondary research, you might use either primary sources, or secondary sources. A *primary source* is one where the author of the published material actually collected the information. For example, a paper written by a scholar who actually conducted the research is a primary source, as is a census report. However, a newspaper article citing either of these primary sources is a *secondary source*. If you are using a secondary source, you are relying on the intermediary—in this example the newspaper reporter—to have transcribed the material accurately. You can see immediately how this might be a problem; however, it is often the only way to gather information. In addition to this obvious problem, technological advances have brought with them new concerns about accuracy and credibility.

Before the advent of the World Wide Web, it was much easier to determine the credibility of sources. The proliferation of online materials from all manner of sources has added another layer of difficulty in determining the credibility of a source. For example, just because a blogger says something is the case, do you believe that individual? Maybe, but it depends on you taking the time to determine the credentials of the source. Add onto this the proliferation of so-called "fake news" sources, and you have significant difficulty in figuring out if you should rely on the information or not. Determining the credibility of your sources is more crucial in the twenty-first century than it has ever been in the past.

In spite of the monikers "primary" and "secondary," secondary research is usually necessary as a first step before primary research can be planned and conducted. Once this secondary source material is collected, the public relations practitioner often needs to conduct **primary research**. In other words, you need to gather first-hand information that is not already available from any other source. The following are examples of *primary public relations research methods*:

- surveys in general

- readership surveys in particular

- focus groups

- interviews

- direct observation.

Figure 2.1 illustrates a typical relationship between primary and secondary sources and their contribution to primary and secondary research. As you can see, both primary and secondary sources are typically required in secondary research, but also in *planning primary research*. There are other relationships that you can probably think of as you acquire research experience, but for now, this is the primary relationship model we'll use.

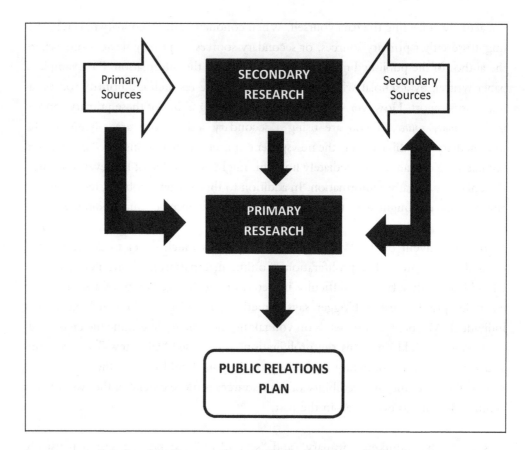

FIGURE 2.1 Relationship Between Source Type and Research Type

MEDIA MONITORING: TRADITIONAL AND SOCIAL

If you know anything about typical data-gathering in public relations already, you might be wondering where *media monitoring* fits in. The information you are collecting is in a secondary source (mass media), but you are using the information collected in a new and unique way; no other organization is likely to be using the same framework as you are for analyzing the information. Thus, for our purposes in public relations, it is useful to consider media monitoring as part of your primary research that is conducted on an ongoing basis, not just in preparation for the development of a program or campaign plan.

Social media monitoring is arguably even more important now than traditional media monitoring; however, it is useful to consider media monitoring as a mandatory part of the overall process of collecting data about how the organization's message (that could include sales, reputation, influence) is perceived publicly. Since you will develop a way to measure the organization's online presence, for our purposes, social media monitoring is part of primary public relations research. (See Chapter 5 for more specifics about social media metrics and monitoring.)

THE PUBLIC RELATIONS/COMMUNICATION AUDIT

One type of public relations research tool that uses both primary and secondary methods for data-gathering is the *public relations/communication audit*. The terms *communication audit* and *public relations audit* are often used interchangeably, although some people in the PR field differentiate between them by suggesting that the public relations audit focuses more on the communication climate within and outside the organization, on the quality of the relationships with publics, and on the role of the public relations function itself. We'll define the communication/public relations audit as follows:

> THE COMMUNICATION/PUBLIC RELATIONS AUDIT **is a research tool that examines and assesses all aspects of an organization's activities, including the internal & external communication climate, to diagnose the extent to which each public is receiving and responding to the messages targeted toward them and the quality of the relationships engendered by the organization through its communication and activities.**

Whenever a public relations practitioner is faced with a new employer, client, or industry, it is almost impossible not to conduct an audit, at least to answer the question: Where are we now?

The data collection carried out in the research phase of the public relations planning process almost always requires a combination of techniques. Thus, before you plunge into the archives or create a survey instrument (see Chapter 6 for further details), you need to create a plan of *how* you are going to research *what* aspects of the organization and its publics, and *why*.

ENVIRONMENTAL SCANNING

From the very beginning of modern public relations practice, understanding the environment within which an organization functions has been an important part of identifying both current and potential PR problems and opportunities. Traditionally, the environmental domains that were important were the political environment (this includes governmental regulations applicable to your business area), the social environment (this includes current public mores and ethical standards), and the economic environment. The twenty-first century has brought with it consideration of a fourth environment: the technological environment. Gathering data about these aspects of the organization's external environment is crucial to effective PR planning.

In her excellent textbook *Planning and Managing Public Relations Campaigns: A Strategic Approach* (included in the resource list in Chapter 6), Professor Anne Gregory provides examples of the kinds of issues that a PR practitioner needs to research when conducting an environmental scan. Some of her suggestions about the kind of data that may be collected while conducting a so-called PEST scan are as follows:

- **POLITICAL DATA**: relevant legislation, changes in government (i.e. political stripe), international political alliances

- **ECONOMIC DATA**: interest rates, unemployment rates, level of disposable income among publics, world business conditions

- **SOCIAL DATA**: population demographics and shifts, educational levels, purchasing habits, social attitudes and concerns

- **TECHNOLOGICAL DATA**: impact of new technologies (e.g. on publics, competitors, partners, employees etc.), current and future technological advances, obsolescence.

If you consider these aspects of an organization's environment, it is probably not difficult to imagine that each of them will have an impact on the organization's ability to cultivate and maintain mutually beneficial relationships—and it is these relationships that are the key to achieving public relations goals and objectives.

SOCIAL MEDIA METRICS

The evolution of social media as a basic communication and influence-building strategy has changed forever the traditional approach to public relations planning which was heavily invested in the concept of "controlling the message." Those days are long gone. The democratization of communication has resulted in the need for PR plans that consider both the potential usefulness of social media as a communication vehicle, as well as the impacts of social media as an uncontrollable medium.

One of the most striking differences between public relations research in the twentieth century and the twenty-first century is the extent to which PR planners are now obliged to focus their data-gathering on internet use by publics. Recent estimates suggest that the average North American who is active on the World Wide Web has upwards of five social media accounts. According to the Pew Center, Facebook continues to be the most popular of all the social media sites, followed by Instagram, Pinterest, LinkedIn and Twitter (see the Pew Center Social Media Update 2016 in Chapter 6). Gathering data from social media platforms and other online activity—your *social media metrics*—helps to shape your understanding of your publics and subsequent public relations projects and campaigns.

The notion of key performance indicators—related to the objectives you set for the campaign/project: e.g. likes and shares, replies and comments (engagement), clicks— is a useful one, but not all of these indicators actually have the same weight in terms of meeting PR objectives. For example, just because people click "like" on your Facebook or Twitter posts this does not translate into any valid measurement of whether or not they are truly engaged with, trust, or support your organization or client. Social media metrics need to be evaluated using a broader framework: specific measurements are useful only in concert with other data you collect during the research phase of developing public relations plans.

It is important, however, for public relations practitioners to be aware that there are many online tools that may assist in the collection of social media data. For example, arguably the biggest and most high-profile of the online tools is Google Analytics. PR professionals can use it to measure a variety of aspects of social media traffic across an array of the organization's online sites. Its metrics can provide information on how your publics behave in relation to your organization or client, and whether or not their engagement translates into the behavior that you are trying to influence via a particular PR plan. The cost for this and other similar services, however, can be steep and the use of this or any other online data-gathering tool needs to be considered in the development of your PR plan's budget. (We'll discuss the budget as a tool for managing implementation in Chapter 4.)

CHARACTERIZING RELATIONSHIPS

One of the "ends" of the research phase is the ability to assess the quality of the relationships that the organization has developed with its publics as a result of proactive and reactive communication and organizational activities. This assessment of the quality of relationships is the first stage of the data analysis.

The answers to the following questions will help the public relations practitioner to characterize the relationships that the organization has with specific publics so that these may be created, maintained, or improved as a result of the subsequent plan:

- What degree of credibility does the organization have in the eyes of this public?

- To what extent does this public understand (a) your mission; (b) your values; (c) your policies?

- To what extent do members of this public believe that they benefit from a relationship with this organization?

- How much conflict has the organization faced with this public recently? In the past?

- How much conflict is the organization likely to face with this public in the future?

- How does this public act toward this organization and what do these actions say about the relationship?

There is little doubt that an organization's relationship with its key publics is fundamental to public relations. However, there is some argument among practitioners about the extent to which relationship measurement can and should be incorporated into the PR research phase. Often the analysis of the relationships is derived from data that has been collected to measure a number of other factors such as repeat customers/clients, employee loyalty rates, number of complaints, and demonstrated online attitudes toward the organization. The quality of the organization's relationships influences all other public relations goals and objectives and should be an underlying metric as you analyse all other data collected.

COMPLETING THE ANALYSIS

Analysis is a key part of the research phase. It is not enough to simply collect the data, you have to do something with it before it becomes useful to you. Unlike the process of *synthesis*, which takes parts of something and forms them into a logical whole, the process of analysis takes the whole of something and breaks it down into its parts. The report about that process is also referred to as an analysis (thus, the term analysis is used as a part of the plan you will write).

The analysis is a significant part of the research phase. Without this process, all you have is a body of information that is both unwieldy and useless. You have to do something with it!

It is often said that individuals either possess an analytical mind or they do not. Learning the skills necessary to analyze data is, however, quite possible. In the practice of public relations, the ability to analyze data and to determine an organization's strengths, weaknesses, problems, and opportunities comes as a result not only of individual talent, but also from experience and judgment. Any good public relations practitioner can develop this talent, and it is a key element of learning to think like a manager.

As you gather data about the organization and its public relations and communication activities, you need to have a way of putting that data into categories and determining the relationships among pieces of data. For example, if you have survey results, you might use *statistics* as part of your analytical process (e.g. averages, standard deviations, chi squares). If you have a series of organizational print materials, you might use the process of *content analysis*. Content analysis can be very informal, or can be a very formalized process of identification and analysis of specific pieces of content. Analyzing print materials might also use the application of any number of available *readability indices* to determine reading level.

One aspect of analysis that is key to figuring out what to do next is to be able to answer the following questions:

- What aspects of the organization's external environment (economic, social, political, technological) are currently affecting it either positively or negatively?

- What aspects of the organization's external environment are likely to affect it in the future?

- How would you describe the organization's internal environment?

- Who are the organization's publics?

- Has the organization accurately identified and described its publics, both current and future?

- How can these publics be categorized?

- How would you characterize the organization's short and long-term relationships with each public?

- What messages does the organization convey to each public?

- Are these the messages that the organization intends to convey?

- What vehicles and channels are used to convey these messages to each public?

- How effectively do these vehicles convey the intended messages? How do you know this?

- To what extent do they convey unintended messages? How do they do this (overtly and subliminally)?

- What organizational actions convey intended and unintended messages to specific publics?

- What are the organization's public relations strengths and weaknesses?

- What are the current public relations problems?

- What are the current public relations opportunities?

The narrative report that discusses all of these questions constitutes what will become the *situational analysis* in the public relations plan. It is important to note that if you are working on a plan that is designed to target one or more specific publics, the foregoing questions need to focus on that aspect of the organization and its environment. For example, if you are developing an internal communications plan, your main focus is on employees and other internal publics (such as volunteers), and only on other publics and the external environment to the extent that these affect your target public.

Using a table as a working tool when you are analyzing the data can be useful. It might look something like the following:

Public(s)	Intended Message(s)	Unintended Message(s)	Current Communication Channels	Analysis

FIGURE 2.2 Basic Data Table

Here is what you should do with each of the columns in this table:

- **Public**: This column is the place where you identify the current publics recognized by the organization. Some of these might include media, the community, employees, clients, customers, volunteers, Board of Directors, governmental agencies, members, and so on. But each is dealt with separately.

- **Message(s) (Intended and unintended)**: These columns enable you to identify the messages that are *currently* being transmitted to the specific publics you have identified. This includes both intended and unintended messages transmitted by either communication or other activities of the organization. Often the messages that the public actually receives and interprets are not the same as those intended by the organization. You need to use the research methods we have discussed to figure this out. In addition, it might be time for the intended message to change.

- **Communication channels**: This is where you examine carefully and delineate the communication channels that are currently being used to disseminate messages or create the organization's image and reputation. Examples of these would include specific social media platforms, newspapers, television, radio, meetings etc. Again, these are categorized according to the specific public identified. For example, your clients might receive most of their information via specific social media channels, while your employees might receive most of their information via face-to-face meetings, but unless you actually gather data about this, you're just guessing. It is also important to remember that organizations use some of their communication channels to reach multiple publics. Even the process of writing blog entries, for example, under a series of publics, might suggest that the organization is trying to accomplish too much with one channel. On the other hand, it may become apparent that one vehicle is not being fully utilized. Again, without research, you are just guessing.

- **Analysis**: This column is probably the most important part of this data table. This is where the analysis really begins. In the Analysis column, you make an initial evaluation of the success or failure of the tool/tactic/vehicle and you begin to discover strengths and weaknesses in the public relations activities of the organization. Here are some questions that you might consider in this column:

  - Does the message that is being transmitted seem appropriate?

  - Is the message an intended one?

  - Are there unintended messages being perceived?

  - Is any message being transmitted at all?

  - Does the vehicle targeted at a particular public seem appropriate?

  - What is the level of the quality of the execution of the tool/tactic/vehicle?

  - Are the messages consistent?

  - Are there any other publics with which the organization ought to have relationships?

  - Is this tool/tactic/vehicle being evaluated at all?

There are two important considerations in using this kind of a tool for data collection and analysis at this stage. First, it is a reflection of the current situation, ***not the situation*** *that you intend to exist after the implementation of a strategic plan.* Second, be aware that it provides you with only a *superficial examination* of the situation at this stage and is not complete enough to examine elaborate two-way communication efforts on the organization's part. This table is useful to you both as you collect data—it can allow you to formulate a visual picture of where you are and what are the relationships among the variables—and it can also serve later as a way to present the data. The table becomes a companion to the narrative portion of the analysis.

Another key aspect of the data analysis is determining the organization's strengths and weaknesses in their communication and relationships with their publics. Finally, from these strengths and weaknesses, the public relations strategist must determine the organization's problems and opportunities (refer back to our definitions and descriptions earlier in the chapter).

Writing up your analysis is the final step. You might consider using the questions posed earlier as a guideline for that written narrative analysis. Once you have your data analyzed, you are ready to move on to the development of your plan. But before you plunge into that planning phase, there is one more important research category important to your plan—especially when you are seeking rationales for your strategy and tactics.

THE IMPORTANCE OF ACADEMIC RESEARCH TO PRACTITIONERS

It often comes as something of a surprise to public relations professionals that there is much to be gained from reading and using results of research published in the relevant scholarly literature. If you know where to look, you will soon discover that the research being conducted and reported by professors in public relations and communications departments at colleges and universities around the world is often relevant, useful, and seriously overlooked.

Let's begin by discussing exactly what academic research is, and how to determine if it is truly useful to you:

> **ACADEMIC (OR SCHOLARLY) RESEARCH is research that is conducted by individuals or groups affiliated with academic institutions for whom part of their job requires them to research and then publish the results of that research.**

The truth is that academic researchers can actually choose just about anything that they want to learn about as the basis of their research. This means that much of what you see published may not appear relevant in the "real world," however, these days it is more likely that researchers in a field like public relations or corporate communications will choose topics that either emanate from or are later relevant to the actual practice of public relations. The problem is that the journals in which they publish may not be readily available to practitioners, and it is still the case that many practitioners don't even know where to look. You should not be among that group.

Since public relations practice draw its theoretical base from a variety of fields including anthropology, psychology, communication studies, and business to name only a few, PR scholars may publish their work in journals in those fields. However, as a starting point it would be useful for you to be familiar with some of the most relevant places where you might find articles of use to you. Here are a few of the most high-profile journals in which you might find useful scholarly research:

- Public Relations Review

- Public Relations Inquiry

- Journal of Professional Communication

- Corporate Communications: An International Journal

- Business Ethics

- Media Ethics

- Journalism and Mass Communication Quarterly

- Journal of Mass Media Ethics

Some of these journals require access through university or college libraries; others are available as open-access online. Either way, it is worth your while to seek them out. Once you access these journals, what will you find?

Let's examine the contents of the November 2016 (Volume 42, Issue 4) issue of *Public Relations Review*, arguably among the most credible of the academic journals in the field. The following are the titles of some of the articles it contains:

- "The Dawn of a New Golden Age for Media Relations? How PR Professionals Interact with the Mass Media and Use New Collaboration Practices."

- "Public Relations and Social Media: Deliberate or Creative Strategic Planning."

- "When the Past Makes News: Cultivating Media Relations through Brand Heritage."

- "Crisis Management at General Motors and Toyota: An Analysis of Gender-specific Communication and Media Coverage."

- "Corporate Social Responsibility, Media Source Preference, Trust, and Public Engagement: The Informed Public's Perspective."

- "Negative Spillover in Corporate–Nonprofit Partnerships: Exploring the Effects of Company–Cause Congruence and Organization–Public Relationships."

So, what can you do with the material that might be contained in these articles? The following questions are practice-based ones that the above-mentioned scholarly studies might help you to answer:

- How can we improve our interaction with local and national media?

- To what extent is our social media done on the fly versus being a planned PR activity?

- How can we use the public's understanding of our history to improve our brand image?

- Should we be communicating differently with different genders?

- What communication channels should we be using to engage our publics with our corporate social responsibility programs?

- How can our not-for-profit organization be prepared to deal with the fall-out from a crisis within one of our sponsor organizations?

These kinds of questions can be directly informed by the results of well-designed and executed academic studies. You can refer to these studies when providing rationales for decisions you have made in the public relations planning process. The next issue to consider is how to read an academic paper.

Once you realize the potential benefits for you as a practitioner and your work of reading and understanding scholarly research, you have opened up a whole set of new ideas.

But an academic article is not the same as a magazine article in *Vogue*, *GQ*, *Men's Health*, or any other magazine that you might read in your leisure time. Scholarly writing has its own framework and is often, sadly, written in a much denser prose than you might be familiar with. That being said, there is really no requirement for you to read every word of the piece in order to understand and be able to use the information it contains.

In general, an academic article contains the following sections:

- Abstract

- Introduction

- Literature Review

- Methodology

- Results

- Discussion

- Conclusions

- References.

There are a few key pieces that you should review, however, and not necessarily in the order in which they are presented. As you review them in the order presented in Figure 2.3, a picture of the usefulness of the research will begin to emerge without you having to slog through every word.

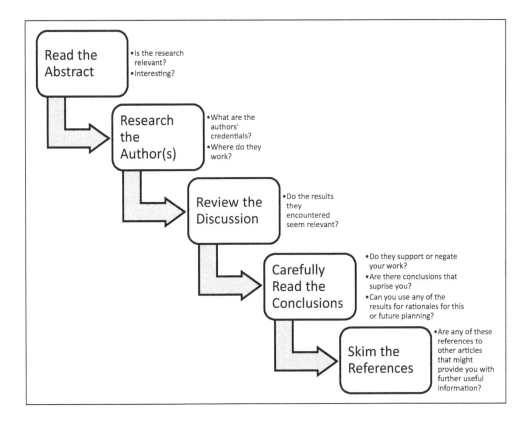

FIGURE 2.3 How to Read an Academic Article

Once you have conducted this kind of an article review, you'll know if you'll be able to use it. If, however, you find that it does not help you to answer your current question, make sure that you don't lose the reference in case you need it in the future.

USING THE WORKSHEETS

The following pages provide you with worksheets that you might find helpful in organizing both your data and your written analysis.

The first is a **DATA TABLE** as we discussed earlier. Use it as you collect your data to identify the publics with whom the organization has relationships, the messages actually communicated and the vehicles, and activities used to communicate those messages. In addition, it provides you the first opportunity to organize your initial assessment of the state of the communication/public relations activities of the organization.

After you have completed the table this far, examine the data again to figure out if there are other publics with whom the organization ought to be developing relationships but is not, and add these to the table. This way of organizing the information will allow you to proceed with the narrative analysis and the determination of strengths and weaknesses.

This leads us to the **PROBLEM AND OPPORTUNITY ANALYSIS** worksheet. Begin with a listing of public relations-related strengths and weaknesses in the left hand column. On the right-hand side, consider corresponding problems and opportunities. This final assessment of problems and opportunities is translated into a narrative description of how you came to determine each one.

The final worksheet for this chapter is the **DATA ANALYSIS CHECKLIST**. Use it initially to determine if you have collected all necessary data. Then, when you have completed your written analysis, use a fresh one as a checklist to evaluate the completeness of your narrative report.

Data Table

Audit Results of Current Public Relations Activities

Public	Intended Message(s)	Unintended Message(s)	Current Communication Channels	Analysis

Problem/Opportunity Analysis

PR Strengths	Potential Opportunities

PR Weaknesses	Potential Problems

Data Analysis Checklist

As you prepare to translate your data analysis into a narrative situational analysis, use the following checklist to ensure that you have collected all relevant information and analyzed it in terms of its relationship to the organization's public relations goals.

- ☐ key aspects of the organization's external environment

- ☐ current and future effects of key elements of external environment

- ☐ key aspects of the organization's internal environment

- ☐ current and future effects of key elements of internal environment

- ☐ identification of publics

- ☐ description of publics

- ☐ consequences of publics for organization and vice versa

- ☐ description of organization's relationships with publics

- ☐ identification of current messages to each public

- ☐ comparison of actual with intended messages

- ☐ identification of vehicles used to convey messages to each public

- ☐ effectiveness of each vehicle in conveying intended messages

- ☐ description of any unintentional messages

- ☐ identification of public relations strengths and weaknesses

- ☐ identification of key public relations problem and/or opportunity

- ☐ extent to which the organization has adapted to environmental pressures

- ☐ extent to which the organization has adapted to changes in its publics

The Planning Phase

VOCABULARY

By the end of this chapter, you should be able to define and discuss the following:

- strategy

- tactic

- communication framework

- communication/public relations strategy

- public relations/ communication goals

- a public

- audience

- stakeholders

- outcome objectives

- process objectives

- public relations core message

- communication vehicles

- social media strategy

THE PLAN

Once the data collection and analysis of the research phase are essentially complete, you have enough information to get you started on the development of a concrete plan to tackle the identified problem(s) and/or opportunity(ies). Keep in mind, however, that although we tend to talk about the four phases of the process as if they were discrete and as if the process itself were linear, in fact it is neither. *Collecting and analyzing data may be necessary throughout the process whenever new information becomes available.* This ongoing process enables you to make corrections as you go along.

There are four key elements to the planning phase. These four elements are as follows:

- defining and describing publics;

- determining the overall goal and specific objectives to get you there;

- articulating the core message and any sub-set of messages for specific publics;

- determining overall strategy, and the tools and tactics that will fit within that strategy.

Before we examine each of these more closely, however, it's important to consider our actual deliverables at the end of this phase. In other words, what are these four elements going to describe when they come together at the end?

One of the deliverables that emanates from this phase is what we'll call a *communication/public relations plan framework*. Like an outline of a more detailed report, this framework sets the groundwork for a more comprehensive strategy. It is a brief glimpse of an organization, its publics, PR objectives, intended messages, vehicles, and approaches, and an overview of how the plan will be evaluated. Every public relations practitioner needs to know how to write such a framework in advance of a detailed plan. It can be used as the outline for writing the more detailed plan document, but it can also be used when you are "pitching" to a client or even your employer. This outline/framework is the first deliverable.

Public relations managers also need to be confident in their abilities to put all of this together as a complete *communication/public relations plan*. This deliverable presents the thoroughly researched, comprehensive plan that delineates clearly the analysis, the problem/opportunity, objectives and communication activities, and evaluation strategies. It involves a detailed analysis of what the organization's relationships are today, where it wants them to be (in three months, one year, five years, for example), and how it will get there. This document is actually written during the planning phase, but considers all four phases of the planning process: research, planning, implementation, and evaluation.

STRATEGIES VERSUS TACTICS

Before we further discuss the pieces that will now go into creating that plan, we need to differentiate between two important concepts: a strategy, and a tool or tactic.

A public relations strategy is the overall approach to getting to the desired outcome; a public relations tactic is the specific vehicle for getting there. For example, if you are trying to increase engagement with your community, the community relations strategy will be based on your research data that would indicate which overall approach to take. It might be the case that you have found that a face-to-face strategy would be most likely to succeed. In that case your tactics might then include such things as town hall meetings, open houses, and opportunities for your employees to participate in community activities while representing your organization. On the other hand, your research might have indicated that a social media strategy might be best, in which case your tactics might include your Instagram account, your Twitter activity and your Facebook page interaction.

Differentiating between your overall strategy and the tactics you'll use to implement that strategy is the first step in really developing a planning mentality that frames all of your thinking about public relations activities.

DEFINING PUBLICS

During the research phase, the public relations practitioner examines the place of the organization within its social, political, economic, and technological environments. At the same time, the publics that have consequences for the organization and for whom the organization has consequences emerge. These publics are obviously groups of people, but for purposes of planning for the public relations needs of organizations, you are going to need a more specific definition.

Over the years, many public relations authors and practitioners have defined publics (refer to any of the general resources listed for Chapter 1 to see examples of these definitions). In practice, we often hear publics defined as groups of people who have a shared interest and are aware of that commonality. On the other hand, it can be argued that members of a public identified by the organization may not be aware of their shared interest or the characteristic they have in common. Other approaches to defining publics could consider geography, socioeconomic status, gender, race, ethnicity, religion, and any other demographic or psychographic factors.

All of these ways of defining publics are useful to public relations practitioners in specific circumstances, but they each have their limitations in practice. Here is a working definition that is useful:

> **A PUBLIC is a group of people who share a common interest, demographic, or psychographic characteristic, as defined by the public relations function of the organization, and whose actions are either influenced by or have an influence on the organization.**

When examining this definition, keep in mind that publics can form on their own in response to organizational activities, policies, or products to pressure the organization. Unless, however, they are eventually identified in the public relations process, they cannot be considered in the strategy. Failing to identify them, either by design or inadvertently, can have major negative consequences for the organization. For example, when creating a five-year strategic public relations plan, you might define your "community" by drawing geographic boundaries. Your neighborhood, your city, your region, or even your entire country might be the community within which you function, and with which you must develop a relationship. On the other hand, an activist group might define itself in response to your organization. They have created the boundaries, but when developing your PR plan, you, too must define them.

Publics can be internal or external. Their activities may currently be influencing the organization or that influence may not yet be felt. They may be ranked in order of priority to the organization (and this is likely to change). If you're dealing with controversy, they may be categorized as *for*, *against*, or *neutral*. It is often useful to use the systems diagram that we discussed in Chapter 1 to plot out the publics and view their relationships with the organization.

The following is a generic list of some of the most commonly described publics:

- employees

- volunteers (in not-for-profits)

- members (in membership organizations)

- financial donors (usually in not-for-profits)

- investors (in publicly held corporations)

- media (traditional mass media, industry-specific media)

- social media including online communities

- community (geographic or otherwise)

- government (various levels)

- regulatory bodies

- consumers/clients (of goods and/or services).

An astute public relations practitioner will be constantly aware of other potential groupings of people that might constitute an important public to the organization at present or in the future. For example, a pharmaceutical company that uses animals in drug research must be constantly aware of animal rights activists in their community. And if there isn't such a group at present, like-minded people could come together for the purpose of targeting the organization. The data collected in the research phase about current publics and the organization's environment provide clues about who the important publics are or should be.

Before we move on to developing objectives for each of your identified publics, let's discuss some relevant terminology that sometimes confuses new public relations practitioners. It is terminology that has become a widespread element of PR jargon. The terms we need to discuss are *audience* and *stakeholder*.

We use the term *public* for a reason. We have defined this particular group in PR terms; an audience on the other hand, is a sub-public: it is a group of people with whom you have one-way communication. Occasionally you might create a public information-type campaign where you do, indeed, consider the public to be a passive *audience*. However, these days even a public information-type strategy usually involves some degree of interaction as a result of social media. Using the term audience when you really mean public can be confusing. For example, if you are the public relations manager for a theater company, you do in fact have an audience: those members of your public who actually sit in the theater seats and watch your plays. They are an important public in and of themselves. However, your donors are not your audience (they may, in fact, also be audience members from time to time, but the relationship you want to maintain with them is broader). Using the term audience implies an unresponsive public with whom there is no two-way communication. Don't use the term unless you mean it.

Then there is the ubiquitous term *stakeholder*. Everyone uses it, from marketers to C-suite office holders, and everyone in between. It really means people who actually hold a share in something. These days, those who use the term argue that our "publics" hold a share in the organization. This is technically not true. In fact, some of our most important publics do not hold any kind of interest in the organization except for opposing them—which, of course is what makes them important publics from a PR perspective. Traditionally, only investors could truly be referred to as stakeholders. The extent to which you can avoid using this jargony term in favor of *public*—which is what we really mean—is important to developing a PR-focused way of thinking.

CONSTRUCTING OBJECTIVES

An ability to construct clear, useful objectives is perhaps the essential key to being an effective planner. You need to know exactly what you intend to accomplish through the activities that will follow.

Although there are many definitions of goals and objectives, let's think of a goal as a broad but pointed statement of what this plan is intended to accomplish. Objectives are the specific outcomes sought for each public being considered in the plan:

> **OUTCOME OBJECTIVES are specific statements of destination that assist in the accomplishment of the stated overall goal. They are clear, measurable, realistic, and include a time frame.**

- *Clear objectives* are stated succinctly, employing language that can be understood by all those who will be involved in the achievement of the outcomes. There should be no argument about their meaning.

- *Measurable objectives* are stated in such a way that the outcome identified can be quantified in some way. This is not always easy but must be attempted. Measurable objectives answer the question: How much of an effect are we seeking? This will eventually allow the PR practitioner to determine the degree of intended effect (success) and to identify those unintended effects that might have resulted from the actions taken.

- *Realistic objectives* recognize that there are limitations to what can reasonably be accomplished given the organization's resources, environmental situations, and time frames.

- Finally, objectives with a *time frame* indicate when the outcome is to be expected: they limit the time for implementation of a plan after which time the approach should be evaluated against the objective itself.

The best way to illustrate outcome objectives is to examine a situation. Consider the case of a not-for-profit membership organization that has been experiencing a downward trend in its membership over the past four years. The research indicates that the external image of the organization is dated and unprofessional, and this is contributing to loss of members and inability to attract new ones. It seems clear, then, that the objectives of the public relations strategy might be to improve the organization's image in the eyes of specific external publics (potential members), and perhaps even with internal publics (current members). That's a useful overall goal that is likely to shore up many aspects of the organization's relationships, but it isn't an outcome objective that meets our criteria. It isn't specific enough and it isn't measurable. Here are two outcome objectives that would contribute to meeting the overall goal of improving or changing the organization's image:

- To increase membership by 30 percent over the next 8 months.

- To retain current members and have them articulate satisfaction with the organization by the end of the year.

The first objective is clear, concise, measurable, and understandable and it includes a time frame for completion. The second one is as well, but it addresses an issue that you will often face. Exactly how do you measure some more nebulous public relations effects such as satisfaction, positive attitude, or image? This objective holds a clue. It indicates that you will measure not satisfaction itself, but articulation of that satisfaction. This kind of objective is useful in another way, too. In it lurks a clue about the kind of tactic or tool you will need to develop. In this case, you will need to devise an opportunity for the current members to respond about this issue. Sometimes the outcome is more qualitative than quantitative and you have to deal with this in as specific a manner as possible.

What is wrong with the following objective?

- To improve the organization's external image by 30 percent.

Not only is this vague (exactly what does an image consist of?), but it is clearly not rational to consider placing a quantitative value on image. In itself, it isn't measurable. Here is a better way of stating the kind of outcome you might be seeking:

- To enhance the organization's image in the community as evidenced by a 50 percent increase in positive reporting about organizational community initiatives in the community newspaper.

Obviously, this objective presupposes that you have counted both the amount and direction (positive or negative) of past coverage of events in this medium.

RELATIONSHIP OBJECTIVES

Public relations is in the business of developing and maintaining relationships with important publics, thus it is necessary to consider not only the communication outcomes but also the relationship outcomes.

Communication outcomes are often framed in terms of knowledge, attitudes, and behaviors that are desirable from a public relations perspective. Obviously, these are important in the development and nurturing of relationships, but recently, public relations has become more interested on the actual quality of the relationships themselves. Modern PR must, as much as possible, try to focus on the kind of relationship that the organization wants and needs to have with its various publics. But how can you develop measurable objectives for something as seemingly nebulous as a relationship?

Although there are no hard and fast rules or even guidelines about this, there are some aspects of relationships that are useful to the public relations effort of the organization. You might consider some of the following questions when formulating these objectives:

- To what extent is it important that this public trust the organization?

- To what extent is it important that this public feel positively about this organization?

- To what extent is it important that this public feel that this organization gives as much as it takes from this public?

Clearly, there are many issues to consider when trying to determine the kind of relationship your organization would like to develop and maintain with publics. These questions will help you to begin to consider relationship outcomes and to include such objectives when developing a public relations plan. If you need further in-depth information on this topic, you can refer to the resource list later in the workbook.

CONSIDERING PROCESSES

Often when you are developing objectives, it is easy to forget that what they really are is an answer to the question: Where do we want to go? Instead, you might fall into the trap of considering only processes. These processes are not ends in themselves, rather, they help to guide the selection and development of communication vehicles. For example, the following objectives are more accurately described as *process objectives* than as *outcome objectives*:

- To communicate regularly with members.

- To post on our Facebook page regularly.

- To ensure timeliness in all communication.

- To enhance opportunities for two-way communication.

Although each of these is admirable, and may even be a necessary part of the objectives of the public relations department in your organization, they are not really strategic. They only speak to the actual process of conducting the public relations and communication activities. Indeed, they are focused more on the PR function rather than on the public. They are very useful objectives if one of the problems you have is the quality of the public relations effort itself. If that is the first PR problem that you identify, then these objectives may be useful as a first step toward the focus you will eventually develop on publics.

KEYING OBJECTIVES TO SPECIFIC PUBLICS

The final issue related to objectives is to consider the intended target of each one. The strongest communication plans key the objectives toward specific publics. For example, in considering media relations, the objectives would be directed specifically toward the media. These objectives about what the public relations planning process aims to achieve are related to what the organization aims to achieve in community relations, employee relations, investor relations, relations with activist organizations, blogger relations, and so on.

Keying objectives to specific publics enables a more directed selection of communication strategies later. Although you might select a particular strategy or vehicle that can achieve more than one objective and is directed toward more than one public, you will eventually need to examine the outcomes for each public separately.

DEVELOPING MESSAGES

Public relations focuses on managing communications between an organization and its publics for the purpose of developing and maintaining long-term, mutually beneficial relationships with those publics. The heart of the PR activity is the message or messages that the organization conveys to its publics in both word and deed. And make no mistake about it, even if the organization does not consciously consider the messages it sends out or develop them purposefully, publics, both external and internal, will see and hear messages all the same and will respond to the organization based on their perception of the messages.

Organizational actions often speak louder than words. It is the responsibility of the public relations function of any organization to ensure that all messages conveyed to various publics are, indeed, the messages that are intended. This naturally presupposes that you've given active consideration to what you really intend to say and that the communication vehicles chosen to convey those messages do so accurately and to the intended public. Thus, at this point in the planning process, once the publics have been identified and the specific objectives for this plan have been set out, the next step is to develop core messages:

> A CORE MESSAGE **is a succinct statement of the core information that the organization intends to convey to its publics with the intended tone.**

Once you have considered the actual core message that you intend to convey via both words and actions, it needs to be considered in the development of every public relations activity that you will develop in an effort to achieve your objectives. Remember, the message has both overt and subliminal aspects, and both are important in the eventual perceptions that arise as a result.

CHOOSING PUBLIC RELATIONS TACTICS AND VEHICLES

The final aspect of the planning phase is selecting appropriate public relations vehicles—the channels and tools that you have reason to believe will successfully convey the intended messages and develop the intended relationships with your publics. The information that you have about your publics—for example, their preferred channels for receiving messages, their level of interest in your organization and its mission, their level of understanding of the issues, their demographics—will help greatly in selecting channels that are most likely to achieve your objectives.

For example, selecting direct mail to disseminate your community relations message is probably not going to be as effective as if you involve your organization in a current community activity or develop a new community activity. Then your actions and the specific communications surrounding those actions will disseminate the message and nurture the relationship.

Here are some things to keep in mind when selecting channels and tools or vehicles:

- This is a creative process. Begin with brainstorming and be open to new ways of looking at old things.

- The tools must be keyed to specific objectives (although one tool might be used to achieve more than one objective, or several tools might be needed to achieve a single objective).

- The channel or tool must be considered in relation to the specific target public.

- You must provide a rationale for selecting both the channel and the tool or vehicle.

Consider first the creative aspect of designing and selecting channels and vehicles. This means that you need to stop thinking in a linear fashion about communication/public relations tools and tactics. A kind of initial brainstorming process allows you to move away from the more familiar strategies to the more creative—perhaps simply a new way of approaching an old strategy. For example, developing a new intranet newsletter may not be the best way to enhance morale among employees. You might consider developing an award that recognizes employees' volunteer activities. The process of nominating and selecting is all part of the communication activity and then the publication of the identity of the winner can even become part of your community relations program.

Also, your first inclination to use mass media (a channel) might be to look for a news angle and disseminate a media release (a tool/vehicle). Even if traditional mass media appear to be the channel of choice in the situation under consideration, there are other tools that you might consider: querying an editor of a feature-type magazine, a newspaper feature, a television interview on a news magazine show, querying a credible blogger, or even paid advertising. Creativity in planning requires that you go beyond your first—and often over-used—inclination. In twenty-first century public relations planning, the focus on social media is often what overshadows other potentially useful channels. Consider all angles.

PLANNING THE SOCIAL MEDIA COMPONENT OF PR PROJECTS

When it comes to overall public relations planning, there are three approaches to the social media planning process:

1. **NO SOCIAL MEDIA COMPONENT**: Although this may seem either old-fashioned or delusional, it is neither. There are public relations planning situations where you may need to back off the social media component. For example, if you have determined that you have an internal PR problem stemming from employees feeling marginalized and distant from upper-level managerial decisions, with a concomitant negative impact on productivity, employing social media in any way may well alienate them even more. This is when PR practitioners have to reach back into traditionalism and find creative ways to rebuild meaningful communication channels. This will likely mean an overall strategy that employs face-to-face news dissemination, town halls, events, and opportunities for your employees. But, you might say, wouldn't it be useful to use social media for letting employees know that these opportunities exist? Maybe, but it would be a lazy approach.

2. **INCLUSION OF SOCIAL MEDIA TOOLS AND TACTICS** (among other tactics): In this situation, the overall strategy is broader than social media, but employing these tools and tactics to disseminate specific messages, to specific publics, to accomplish specific objectives is appropriate and demonstrates best practice. In fact, considering social media in this way is the most common approach to using these tools in modern public relations and communication planning.

3. **THE SOCIAL MEDIA CAMPAIGN**: Sometimes it's clear that the organization or client's social media presence is the problem in and of itself. Then the PR plan can and should be the development of an overall social media strategy using social media tools and tactics. The truth is that social media is so important these days that large organizations employ people to work within the social media strategy exclusively. Even in these situations, though, fundamental public relations planning is important. For example, the social media strategy plan begins with research as we have detailed, followed by setting measurable objectives, which are then fulfilled by strategic selection of social media tools and tactics. In the end, the strategy also needs to include measurement of results—the evaluation.

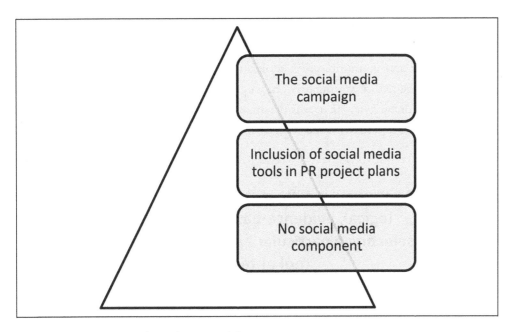

FIGURE 3.1 The Social Media Pyramid

You'll note that in Figure 3.1, the PR project plan that lacks any social media capacity whatsoever is the basis of the pyramid, rather than the other way around. It's important to understand that public relations and communication planning, whether it includes social media in part or even in total, needs to begin with the fundamentals of the PR process.

If you consider the social media planning process presented in Figure 3.2, you'll begin to understand that it is a variation of the PR planning process itself.

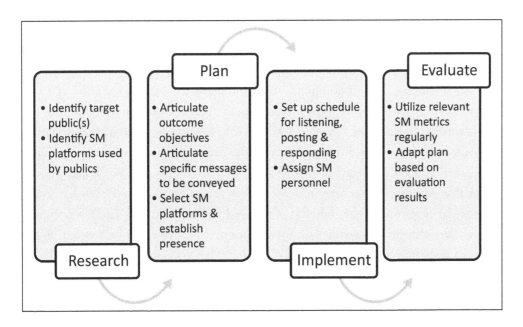

FIGURE 3.2 The Social Media Planning Process

RATIONALES FOR CHANNELS AND STRATEGIES

Public relations and communication tools and tactics that are not keyed to specific objectives run the risk of wasting time, money, and effort. Why would you implement a communication activity that wasn't strategically designed to achieve a specific objective? This is tied in with the issue of rationale:

> A RATIONALE is a clear statement providing logical, evidence-based reasons for selecting a particular approach, strategy, tool or tactic.

The rationale you provide needs to address the extent to which you are confident this approach will achieve the desired results, and the basis of that confidence. Before you decide on a particular approach to solving a problem or capitalizing on an opportunity, you need the answers to the following questions:

- What makes you believe that this approach you are proposing is likely to work with this particular public?

- Can this combination of channel and vehicle actually accomplish your objective(s)?

- What external basis or past experience do you have upon which you can defend this decision?

You need a strong basis in communication and audience-analysis theories, and you need to keep up with what is going on in the field. (Review our discussion of industry and academic research in Chapter 1.) The inherently empirical nature of public relations—in other words, it relies largely on the extent to which we have experience with a particular approach rather than on some scholar's theory of what should work—means that you can learn a lot from case studies presented in both the academic and the popular literature of the industry. You need to keep current. The development of rationales also provides you with a basis upon which you can lean when you're trying to convince employers and/or clients that what you are proposing actually has some chance of working.

SUMMARIZING THE PLANNING STAGE

Since there are many moving parts in the planning phase, it is worthwhile taking a few minutes to visualize them together as a process. Figure 3.3 provides this summary so that you can review the complete planning phase before moving on to the step wherein you manage the implementation of your plan.

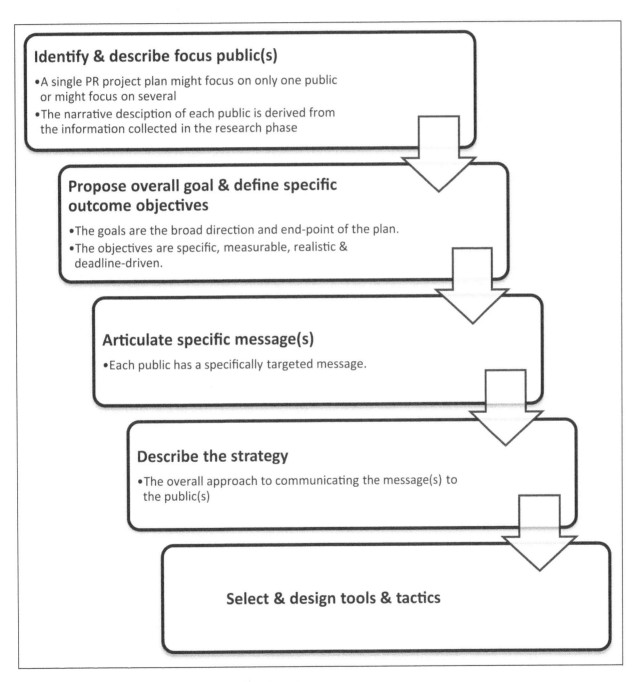

FIGURE 3.3 Summary of Steps in the Planning Phase

USING THE WORKSHEETS

There are three worksheets accompanying this chapter.

The first is **IDENTIFICATION AND CATEGORIZATION OF PUBLICS**, which is designed to help you to identify the publics that you will be focusing on for this particular plan. The decision about these publics will be drawn from your research data, both the current publics with whom the organization has relationships as well as those with whom it should. Sometimes, you may have only one public if this is a small plan designed to accomplish a very specific, time-limited goal. The systems-like chart will give you a visual representation of the relationships between the organization and its relevant publics as well as a chance to consider environmental pressures and the type of communication.

The second worksheet is a **CHECKLIST FOR OUTCOME OBJECTIVES**. Especially when you first begin to develop objectives, it's useful to have such a checklist to evaluate their quality before you move on.

The third worksheet pulls all your previous work together as a **PUBLIC RELATIONS PLAN** worksheet. It puts together in chart form the plan that you are creating. It keys messages to publics, to objectives, to channels and tactics, to the accomplishment of specific objectives. Use this as a first step in determining strategic approaches and to visualize the connections between objectives, publics, and approaches to make the best use of each.

The final worksheet focuses on **SOCIAL MEDIA**. It is specifically designed to assist you at the planning stage in identifying how you might use individual social media platforms to achieve specific goals.

Identification and Categorization of Publics

Categorize and rank publics in terms of their relationship with the focal organization and the environment.

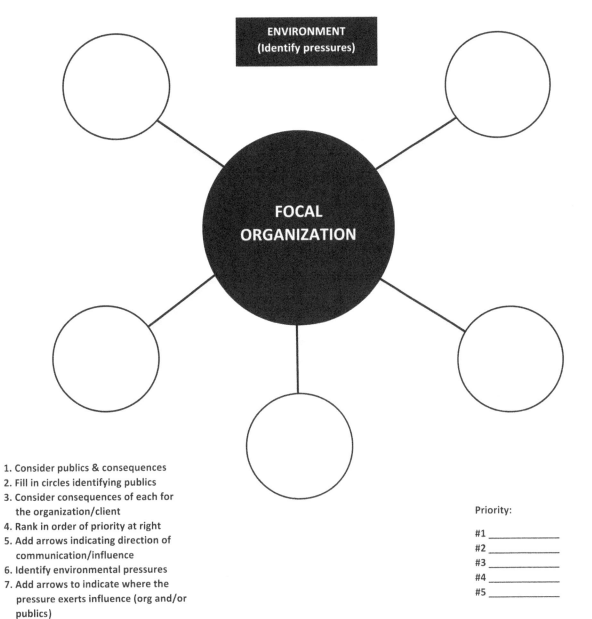

ENVIRONMENT
(Identify pressures)

FOCAL ORGANIZATION

1. Consider publics & consequences
2. Fill in circles identifying publics
3. Consider consequences of each for the organization/client
4. Rank in order of priority at right
5. Add arrows indicating direction of communication/influence
6. Identify environmental pressures
7. Add arrows to indicate where the pressure exerts influence (org and/or publics)

Priority:

#1 _____
#2 _____
#3 _____
#4 _____
#5 _____

Checklist for Outcome Objectives

To evaluate the quality of your objectives

☐ The wording is clear and concise.

☐ The members of this organization will understand this objective.

☐ The stated outcome is realistic.

☐ The stated outcome is feasible for this organization, at this time.

☐ There is an explicit date for completion.

☐ The stated outcome is measurable.

☐ The stated outcome is a communication/public relations effect.

Public Relations Plan Worksheet

Articulate your overall message and your specifically derived messages, objectives, and targeted tools and tactics for each public. This is the template for your plan/outline.

Overall Message for this Project/Campaign

Public #1	Public #2	Public #3	Public #4
Message	Message	Message	Message
Objectives 1. 2. 3.	Objectives 1. 2. 3.	Objectives 1. 2. 3.	Objectives 1. 2. 3.
Tools & Tactics:	Tools & Tactics	Tools & Tactics	Tools & Tactics

Social Media Worksheet

Use this checklist to identify applications for individual social media platforms

Platform	Potential Application
☐ **Facebook**	☐ Organizational announcements ☐ Behind-the-scene photos ☐ Inspirational quotes ☐ Polls ☐ Reposts of blog links ☐ Other _____
☐ **Blog**	☐ Long-form (800-1000 word) features ☐ Interaction with readers
☐ **Twitter**	☐ Linked to Facebook posts as above ☐ Industry-related news ☐ Live updates during events/media conferences ☐ Calls to action ☐ Retweets of relevant follower tweets ☐ Response to incoming tweets ☐ Other _____
☐ **Pinterest**	☐ Product photos ☐ Follow competition ☐ Other _____
☐ **LinkedIn**	☐ Recruitment ☐ Organizational news ☐ Industry news ☐ Other _____
☐ **Instagram**	☐ Product photos ☐ Photos telling the organization's story ☐ Other _____
☐ **Other platform (Google +, Quora, FourSquare etc.)**	☐ _____ ☐ _____

CHAPTER 4

Managing Implementation

VOCABULARY

By the end of this chapter, you should be able to define and discuss the following:

- control
- influence
- management
- leadership
- delegation

- budget
- Gantt chart
- flow sheets
- quality control

REVISITING MANAGEMENT DEFINITIONS

Implementation of the public relations plan is the third step of the public relations process. It implies carrying out the activities developed in the planning step. For the public relations technician, that's all there is to know. From a technical perspective, it is now time to get to work on carrying out the technical aspects of the plan. But for the public relations manager, a crucial part of the management process is just beginning.

We began our attempt to define management in Chapter 1. We discussed the fact that there are as many definitions of management as there are people writing about the subject. Now as we move into the practical application of the concept, the following commonalities of the definitions emerge as key to our understanding:

- Management is a process.

- Management involves and concentrates on reaching the organization's goals.

- Management involves working with and through people.

- Management involves working with and through organizational resources.

We can see from these aspects of management that, in general, managers are concerned with managing people, financial resources, time, and quality.

The first aspect of this definition means that management is not a "thing" and it is not static. It continually changes because it involves a series of continuing and related activities. Management is clearly not something that you do once in a while. It is continuous.

Next, management of the organization focuses on reaching *organizational goals*. For the public relations function, this means ensuring that any public relations strategies developed are in line with the overall goals of the organization. The communication and public relations activities are not ends in themselves, rather, they contribute to the organization's bottom line.

Managers must have highly evolved "people" skills. If managing the public relations process means managing the activities of people, it means that the manager needs to be able to develop good rapport, assess the strengths and weakness of the staff, *delegate* appropriate activities to appropriate staff members, assess the work accomplished, and enhance the working environment by creating a climate of cooperation and collaboration.

Managers also need knowledge and skills in organizing other resources of the organization. These include primarily time, money, and quality. Tools that managers use to manage these resources include **budgets**, **flow sheets**, and **time and activity management charts**.

Historically, there have been many disagreements about how best to analyze and react to management situations. Early in the twentieth century, many of those studying management as a discipline were focused on the actual activities that the workers performed. Most management theorists focused on the one best way to carry out a job, whether it was shoveling coal or laying bricks. These "management consultants" were quite successful in helping organizations of various sorts to decrease the number of people required to do this physical labor and to increase their profit margins. There was little concern, however, about the people aspect of the job.

THE HISTORICAL CONTEXT

Other consultants examined this classical approach to management and decided that the human factor needed more consideration. These theorists injected such elements as employee morale and motivation into the management systems and came up with ways that organizations could adapt themselves to their people. Such work paved the way for systems of reward to be used to enhance the work an individual was prepared to perform for an employer.

Other approaches to management include the more recent management science approach, which borrows from mathematical and scientific techniques that include observation, deduction and testing, and the development of ways of dealing with contingencies. One approach to management theory that we have already examined is the systems approach. Since this approach involves examining relationships, it is a very useful framework for applying to the management of public relations (see Chapter 1).

Before we move on to specific aspects of how to manage the implementation of a project, we need to examine the relationship between management as a general concept, and the concept of leadership. To the casual observer, they may appear to be one and the same; in fact they are quite different in both focus and skills required.

MANAGEMENT AND LEADERSHIP

Leaders are those visionaries who can visualize the future and where the organization should be heading. Great leaders can communicate that vision to their followers and gain their support and "buy-in." The managers may set the more short-term goals that lead toward the vision, and are able to communicate those goals to co-workers, gaining their support and buy-in for the approach to achieving those short-term goals:

MANAGEMENT ensures the day-to-day accomplishment of organizational activities designed to move the organization in the direction of its ultimate goal.

LEADERSHIP is the force that determines direction and ultimate goal.

In any discussion of leadership and management the question always arises of whether managers are leaders and whether leaders need to be managers. There is no universal answer to these questions, but logic leads us to conclude that managers need not be leaders in the visionary sense (although it wouldn't hurt), but need to be able to lead people in day-to-day activities. Any group of people working together needs working leadership to assign tasks, arbitrate in conflicts, and evaluate activities. The manager in this position also provides the communication link between the workers and the leadership of the organization.

On the other hand, a great leader may not be a great manager. This leader may be completely versed in the issues and trends in the organization's external environment, exhibiting all the hallmarks of a true futurist, but be relatively inept at the day-to-day activities required to manage a project. Would it be useful for a leader to be a good manager? Of course it would be helpful if this individual had experience in more junior management positions in an organization, if for no other reason than to enhance his or her credibility in the eyes of the followers. But when leaders regularly involve themselves in those day-to-day management activities, it can cause problems both for the managers whose jobs they are intruding on and for the long-term vision of the organization. It's difficult, if not impossible, for a great leader to be future-focused when enmeshed in the daily grind of managing projects.

BUDGETS AS MANAGEMENT TOOLS

Let's begin our discussion of management tools with an examination of budgeting, since this is likely the first step you will need to take in managing the implementation of the public relations plan. More than any other aspect of managing projects, budgeting seems to frighten public relations practitioners. In reality, though, if you're like the rest of us you've probably been acquiring experience with budgeting since you were very young.

If your parents provided you with an allowance, you soon recognized that it would only go so far. If you wanted to buy something special with your allowance and you didn't have enough money, you had to make a decision. Either you would wait until you did have enough money, or you allocated your available resources in a different way. Perhaps you settled for a less expensive item, or even two less expensive items. In any case, you already know something about allocating financial resources.

As you got older, your expenses likely grew, but then so did your income. Thus, even if you believe yourself to be hopeless in sticking to a personal budget, you've probably had occasion to examine your income on the one hand versus your expenses on the other. This encompasses the basic concepts of budgeting:

> **A BUDGET FOR A PUBLIC RELATIONS project is a financial plan for allocating specific sums of money to specific activities required for the achievement of the objectives. It is a management tool.**

Thus a budget performs two main functions: it is a control mechanism for the activities necessary to achieve the objectives, and it is a communication tool to explain public relations activities and objectives to non-PR managers and other organizational leaders.

In public relations, there are two general categories of budgets that we deal with. The first is a *program budget* or *project budget*. It is a more global way to think about the allocation of financial resources in the public relations activities of an organization. It refers to a specific sum of money that is allocated to cover a program or project, and considers the public relations activities in a holistic way. This contrasts with a *line item budget* where the public relations function is budgeted by allowing the department specific sums for items such as printing, design services, postage, couriers, office supplies, and so on. This is a more piecemeal way to budget for public relations activities. If, however, your departmental budget *is* a line item budget, you have no alternative in project budgeting but to use those same items and budget them into the project in that way. This approach sometimes makes it more difficult to include new items that may not be in the departmental item list and to reallocate budgeted proportions for specific items.

When faced with a program budget for public relations activities, the general approach to budgeting the specific project is to assign a sum of money as a project budget. That sum is then broken down to cover the activities that are required by the plan you have already developed. It should be clear at this point that considerations about budgets should also be made during the planning phase so that you are not now faced with champagne activities planned on a beer budget, as the saying goes.

The project manager then takes the public relations plan already developed and breaks it down into specific activities and items that need to be covered in order to achieve the objectives. The following are some of the things that you need to consider in the initial development of a realistic, accurate budget:

- Who will be involved in the overall implementation?

- What specific tasks will each person be assigned to complete?

- Realistically, how long will it take each person to complete his or her tasks?

- What materials will be required?

- What outside services will be required (such as printers, couriers, postage, models, actors, studio time, social media monitoring services, photographers, audio-visual services, room rentals, equipment rentals)?

- Do you have estimates of costs from all required outside services?

Once all of these are taken into consideration, you'll need to compare the grand total to the budgeted amount and revise as necessary. It takes professional judgment to consider where money can be saved and where it needs to be maintained to still be able to accomplish the objectives. Sometimes it is necessary to rethink some aspects of the objectives (are they still realistic given the resources available?), or the communication vehicles selected (is there another effective vehicle that we can use and still stay within budget?).

The manager is also responsible for determining at which points it will be feasible to reexamine the budget, in process, to ensure that the project is still on target. This allows the budget to become another control tool.

DEADLINES AND TIME MANAGEMENT

Managing time means managing *people's* time. It means being able to schedule activities so that the project comes in not only on budget, as we discussed previously, but **on deadline**. Public relations practitioners are well aware that the ability to meet deadlines is crucial to the successful practice of PR. As such, individual public relations practitioners may be fully aware of how long it takes them to carry out specific tasks and thus meet those deadlines. The public relations manager, on the other hand, must estimate how long it will take any number of people to carry out any number of tasks, and create a schedule that considers both people and project requirements. An important project requirement is the prerequisite nature of some of those activities. In other words, some activities must be completed, or at least in progress, before others can be started. The manager needs to juggle all of these.

Public relations managers use a variety of tools to schedule time. The simplest is the one that many people use for personal time management; it is the to-do list. These laundry lists of activities are useful but have serious limitations. They don't consider priorities, how long each task will take, or if any are prerequisites to others. These kinds of to-do lists, whether electronic or on paper, are also useful only for individual time-planning, not managing team projects. Thus, as a management tool they are only the first step toward controlling deadlines. What you really need is some kind of action plan that organizes those activities.

The **Gantt Chart** is one tool that managers in general have been using since early in the twentieth century when management consultant Henry Gantt developed it. In simple terms, a Gantt chart takes that laundry list of activities and places them on a chart that has activities down one side and time lapse across. It then uses bars to plot out the time it will take to complete each individual task, considering when the activity should be started and how it may overlap other activities. The chart is a plan for time management and just as a budget can be used during the course of the project to determine the extent to which you are likely to stay on budget, the Gantt chart can be used to determine whether or not you are likely to meet your deadline. One of the most important aspects of the Gantt chart, however, is that it isn't carved in stone. If it looks like the plan will not allow you to bring the project to a conclusion on time, then the schedule must be changed and you need to update your chart.

Figure 4.1 illustrates what a simple Gantt chart might look like.

Developing a Gantt chart these days is easier than ever. Software programs are widely available and allow you to begin by inserting your list of activities and their sub-activities into a spreadsheet. Then the program creates the chart for you.

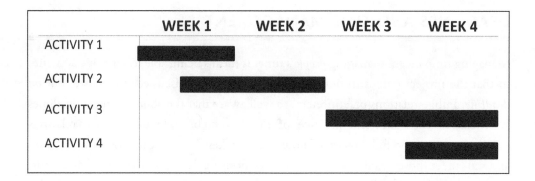

FIGURE 4.1 Simple Gantt Chart

The generic example in Figure 4.1 shows that activity #1 begins at the beginning of week 1 and will be finished by the beginning of week 2. The beginning of activity #2 overlaps with activity #1 and is complete by the end of week 2. This completion is necessary before activity #3 can begin. Activities #3 and #4 should be complete by the end of the 4-week project.

As you probably already have figured out, the ability to prepare an accurate and useful Gantt chart, or any other tool for managing time, presupposes that you have the ability to estimate how much time it will take to complete any given task. This is when a manager's previous experience as a public relations technician is extremely useful. If, however, you have never actually carried out the task you are assigning to someone else, you'll need to consult with someone who does have this experience. It is foolhardy to estimate the time required based on nothing more than your gut feeling.

In addition to this professional experience and judgment, there are actually mathematical models for estimating time. To use these, however, requires that you have a sense of both the most optimistic (but realistic) time projection as well as the most pessimistic (but realistic) time projection. The math involves calculating just where that most likely time is: it falls somewhere between the most pessimistic and the most optimistic.

It is well known that most activities tend to take longer than anticipated. For example, everyone complains about construction deadlines never being met. It seems that there is a significant amount of evidence to support this notion. However, taking a few steps when planning your project will assist you in estimating the time required for the completion of individual tasks as well as projects overall. Figure 4.2 summarizes these steps.

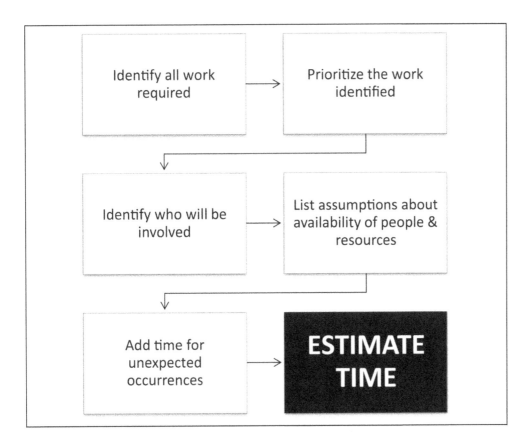

FIGURE 4.2 How Long Will that Take? Steps for Estimating Time

MAINTAINING QUALITY CONTROL

Now that we have examined the overall concept of management, and have considered the management of both time and financial resources, another parameter we need to consider is the management of quality as the project progresses.

There's a lot of talk today about quality assurance, quality control, total quality management, to mention a few of the buzzwords. Overall, unlike in the days of the so-called Robber Barons of the early twentieth century when big business cared only for its own estimate of its quality, most organizations today are committed to the concept of comprehensive, consumer-focused programs of *quality management*. This is embodied in the notion of TQM (total quality management), which provides an organization with a competitive edge. Managing the quality of a specific public relations project, then, is part of the organization's overall commitment to quality. As the manager of the public relations project, it's your responsibility to find a way to monitor and control the quality.

The first step happens during the planning process. As you select and develop the outcome objectives for the project, you are actually saying that this is the level of outcome you'll achieve. During the final or evaluation phase of the project, you'll figure out if you've met those objectives. At that point you'll be able to say that you did or did not achieve the kind of quality outcome you were planning on. As the project progresses, however, you do need to be aware of the level of quality of the work and the interim outcomes to avoid any surprises at the end.

Some of the parameters that you might consider as on-going measures of quality of the public relations output are as follows:

- consistency

- reliability

- accuracy

- congruence

- honesty

Let's examine each of these parameters to determine the extent to which they might be useful for you to build into your quality monitoring plan. Keep in mind that they are specific to the public relations effort of the organization. If you were monitoring the quality of a manufacturing effort, the quality measures would be different.

CONSISTENCY: One of the most important aspects of any organization's messages to its publics is that they be consistent. These messages are carried in both the organization's actions as well as its overt messages. For example, there is both a conscious and a subliminal message carried in the corporate identity program. Are these messages consistent? Are these aspects of this particular project consistent with the organizational norm as well as with one another? Has the creative impulse led you astray? Do all aspects of this particular project carry a consistent style and message?

RELIABILITY: This refers to the ability of the organization's public relations thrust to do what it says it will do. In general, this would refer to the PR department's ability to achieve its overall objectives. In the case of the specific public relations project, do the activities continue to move the project toward successful completion of the objectives set? Are these the kinds of activities that will actually assist the department in achieving its overall goals?

ACCURACY: This is an extremely important aspect of quality of the public relations output of any organization. Are all aspects of this project accurate? Is all of the information posted on your social media accounts accurate? Does the photo selected for the media kit accurately display the message intended? Has someone checked all the statistics mentioned in the news release? A public relations project can succeed or fail on the accuracy of the information presented. There is nothing worse than finding an error in content that has already been transmitted to your publics. Even worse is when a member of a public finds it before you do. This is more important than ever these days given the rapidity of reposting online material. You may delete or edit a tweet, for example, but it is likely too late.

CONGRUENCE: This refers to the extent to which all of the aspects of the program "fit" together. Are the parts harmonious? Do they agree with one another? The estimate of ongoing congruence may be based on such concrete aspects as the design parameters (having only one designer can help with this), or on such esoteric things as your overall professional judgment.

HONESTY: Clearly, honesty is a value that is held in high esteem in communi-cations professions such as public relations. As a final ongoing check of the quality of a public relations effort, you need to determine the extent to which the project is projecting the messages honestly, and in a way that does not result in misleading the public.

These are overall quality parameters in public relations. For individual aspects of programs, you may be able to develop more specific ones. This is merely a starting point.

MANAGING PEOPLE: WORKING WITH AND THROUGH

As we began our discussion of management, we defined it partially as working with and through people. The final aspect of managing the public relations project is managing the people involved. Sometimes, you are the only person involved. Other times, the other people with whom you will work during the course of a project are outside designers, printers, and others. But frequently, you will have one or more other public relations people working with you on this project. As the manager of the project, you are responsible for getting the most out of those people while assisting them to maintain their morale and motivation.

Delegation is one of the most important and most frequently discussed people skills in managing projects:

> **DELEGATION is entrusting another individual with the authority to make decisions about and carry out a specific activity. Delegation is usually from one level on the organizational chart to a lower one.**

Delegation does not mean getting rid of the jobs that you don't want to do. It means determining the best person for the job and giving that person the responsibility and authority to do it. Clearly you need to know the strengths and weaknesses of the people with whom you are working, and you need to use these to your best advantage. If you are loathe to delegate, then you need to examine your own motivation and consider why you have difficulty giving up specific tasks. A manager who cannot delegate will have significant operational and staff problems.

Delegation, however, also means that you need a regular means to communicate with these people on an ongoing basis so that you can maintain control of the project without taking away a certain degree of autonomy. Regular team meetings can be helpful, but individual meetings are also useful in maintaining control. Most management textbooks devote a significant amount of time to the skill of delegation. Refer to the reading list for more information.

USING THE WORKSHEETS

There are three worksheets for this chapter. They are designed to assist you in managing the three most common managerial parameters: financial resources, time, and quality.

Use the first worksheet the **BUDGET WORKSHEET** which is designed as a basic tool to assist you in the first stages of planning for allocation of the financial resources for the project. In Section 1, identify those individuals within your organization who will be charged with various specific responsibilities for this project. Begin with your own activities, your hourly rate, the projected number of hours you will spend and determine the total cost of your services. Then repeat this process for every individual who will be involved. Remember to include clerical, administrative, and other technical support.

Section 2 of the budget worksheet requires you to consider all outside services that this project will necessitate. Here you would consider printing, photography, courier, studio rentals, catering, and the like. Before you can estimate these costs though, you'll need actual estimates from each of these people. You might even have requested such estimates from more than one source to ensure the best price.

Section 3 is where you list the materials that will be required for this project. If you are planning an event, for example, you'll need to consider every small detail such as name tags, pens and pencils for the delegates, and markers for the flipcharts if you still use them (unless the venue provides these, but you'll need to know). Also include an amount for out-of-pocket expenses: everyone forgets small things, such as parking for the guest speaker, from time to time!

The second worksheet is like a traditional Gantt chart for **TIME MANAGEMENT**. Follow the instructions in the left-hand column and remember to revise your time management chart as the project progresses. Even if you don't always prepare a chart like this for implementation, it is a useful exercise to do it once in a while to ensure that you are still able to break down an activity into its constituent tasks and to estimate the time it will take for completion of each.

The final worksheet to use during the implementation phase, is the **QUALITY CONTROL CHECKLIST**. You may need to use more than one of these to assess the quality of specific aspects of the plan.

Budget Worksheet

A simple, first-pass tool to prepare a preliminary budget

Section 1: Activities & Person Hours

Activity	Responsibility	Rate	Hours	Total

Total projected cost/person hours $_____

Section 2: Outside Services

Service Provider	Description of Service	Cost

Total projected cost/outside services $_____

Section 3: Materials

Materials Source	Description	Cost

Total projected cost/materials $_____

GRAND TOTAL $_____

WORKSHEET 4.2

Time Management
Prepare a simplified Gantt Chart

INSTRUCTIONS

1. Prepare a complete list of activities required to compete the relevant part of the plan.
2. List "activities" as items on vertical axis.
3. Place an X at the time point where the activity must begin.
4. Place an X at the time point for deadline for completion.
5. Join the X's with a straight line.
6. Repeat for each activity.
7. Note that there will be overlaps in activities.

Activity

1. _____
2. _____
3. _____
4. _____
5. _____
6. _____
7. _____
8. _____

☐ days   ☐ weeks   ☐ months

Quality Control Checklist

Review this checklist for each of the activities in your plan.

Consistency Measures

- ☐ messages are consistent
- ☐ tone is consistent
- ☐ style is consistent

Reliability Measures

- ☐ each element moves toward overall goal
- ☐ elements together move toward organizational goals

Accuracy Measures

- ☐ content is accurate
- ☐ materials are error-free

Congruency Measures

- ☐ elements all "fit"
- ☐ there are no apparent, unexplained 'outliers'

Honesty Measures

- ☐ message content is truthful
- ☐ message content is not misleading
- ☐ message delivery is not misleading

CHAPTER 5

Evaluation

VOCABULARY

By the end of this chapter, you should be able to define and discuss the following:

- formative research
- summative research
- measurement
- quantitative measurement
- qualitative measurement

- media monitoring
- social media monitoring
- benchmarking
- reputation
- "The Barcelona Principles"

A PRACTICAL DEFINITION

Evaluation is both an end and a beginning. Although this phase seems to bring up the rear of the four steps in the public relations process (research, plan, implement, evaluate), it should also be considered a beginning. And as such, it is arguably the most important step:

> **EVALUATION is a measurement of an organization's success in disseminating planned messages to its targeted publics to reach specific communication and relationship goals and objectives.**

Evaluation is first and foremost another research phase. Research that you conduct at the beginning of the planning process is properly referred to as *formative research*. Research that you do in an effort to evaluate a PR project is called *summative research*. Summative research, however, also becomes part of the data that you will likely use in future projects: at that point it becomes formative research.

Thus, the data collected in an effort to measure the success or failure of any aspect of a public relations campaign or program are analyzed to provide useful information during the research phase of the next part of the program. It's like a circular feedback loop.

If you think of it as a cycle as presented in Figure 5.1, you begin to understand that the research and evaluation phases of PR planning are linked through ongoing data collection, which is a continuous part of the implementation of any PR or

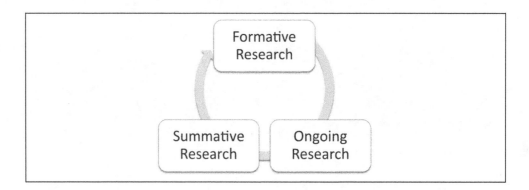

FIGURE 5.1 The Evaluation Cycle

communication activity. This means that research—data collection and analysis—of one sort or another is a continuing and on-going process in public relations planning.

This chapter is about how to plan for evaluation of the public relations project. For more detailed information regarding how to carry out any of the specific types of evaluation strategies, you'll need to refer to the resource lists in Chapter 6 (although many strategies are quite self-evident and need no special skills). The evaluation, then, is planned at the time that the project itself is planned, and it is only as valid as the objectives. We'll come back to this as we discuss the validity and complexity of what is often evaluated in public relations practice.

WHY EVALUATE AT ALL?

Historically, public relations has been known by what people can actually see—in other words what is actually implemented. The fact that what is implemented needs to be evaluated might seem self-evident in this age of accountability, but it is still not a foregone conclusion that everyone sees the need to evaluate what public relations does in any meaningful way. Many people who are not schooled in the field seem to feel that a "gut" reaction is sufficient; or that simply keeping track of how much work is done constitutes evaluation. Modern public relations and business practices take issue with these unsubstantiated or superficial approaches.

Years ago, a guest speaker in one of my first-year public relations classes presented a case study of a public relations campaign that had been implemented by the department of which he was a part. Much to these neophyte students' delight, he presented all of the materials that had been used to disseminate a very well-thought-out message to a very specific target public. When asked about the success of the program, he happily reported that it had been a stellar success. I thought of this as a good opportunity for students to see evaluation in action, so I asked him to tell the students how they had determined the success of the program. He said: "Everyone liked the posters!"

If the objective of the communication exercise had been to have everyone like the posters, then one would have no choice but to deem it a success. The objectives, however, would have been flawed and thus the outcomes just as flawed from a public relations perspective. This, however, is what I've come to term the *happiness index*, and it isn't nearly as extinct an evaluation tool as it ought to be.

We need to evaluate public relations programs for many of the same reasons that we need to do research before we begin planning. This kind of happiness index is not helpful.

THE "BARCELONA PRINCIPLES"

In 2010 the professional public relations industry took a major step forward when a set of principles governing public relations and communication measurement were established by the *The International Association of Measurement and Evaluation of Communication* at a meeting in Barcelona, Spain. The seven principles that were adopted by 33 participating countries represented a high-profile acknowledgement of the important role that measurement plays in the modern practice of public relations.

Figure 5.2 presents the seven principles, as updated in 2015, in summary.

It's important to evaluate outcomes, outputs and organization impacts.
You should employ both quantitative and qualitative methods.
All strategies and tactics, including social media, need to be measured.
You should use only transparent, consistent and valid measurements.

FIGURE 5.2 Summary of the "Barcelona Principles"

A careful examination of these principles makes it clear that measurement—the key to evaluation—is a part of all phases in the planning process as we discussed above. It also lends credence to the notion that PR and communication are important, bottom-line functions within organizations in the twenty-first century.

WHAT WE EVALUATE

Just as in the selection of communication vehicles and channels, the selection of evaluation techniques and tools offers an opportunity for creativity. This creativity, however, is always tempered by the constraints inherent in the objectives of the plan. Thus, the goal here is to select evaluation tools that will measure exactly what you intend to measure in the public in which you intend to measure it.

Through the years, public relations managers have taken a variety of approaches to evaluation, not all of them useful, as we already have alluded to. Before you can create an evaluation plan, you need to consider the possibilities of what can actually be measured, how valid that measurement will be, and the feasibility of you being able to carry out the particular evaluation process.

What you evaluate is as telling about your professional judgment as your ability to select effective communication vehicles and approaches.

Here are some of the aspects of the public relations program that can be measured:

- how productive you've been;

- how far afield you've disseminated your message(s);

- the accuracy of the message(s) disseminated;

- whether anyone in your target public saw/heard the message;

- change in knowledge level of your target public;

- change in attitude of your target public;

- change in behavior of your target public;

- change in the quality of the relationship between this public and your organization (including online engagement).

Let's examine each of these in more detail so that you will be able to consider whether or not you would select a tool based on one of these general approaches.

HOW PRODUCTIVE YOU'VE BEEN: This is easy. If you want to know how productive you've been, you simply keep a tally of the work that's done during the implementation phase of the project. How many media releases did you write? How many interviews did you arrange? How many press conferences took place? How many tweets did you post? Although there may be a good reason for keeping track of your productivity in this way (to bill clients, for example), there is little justification for using any of these approaches to evaluate the public relations project. This approach lacks validity in that it does nothing to measure communication/relationship outcomes at all. *Just because you did a lot of work, does not necessarily translate into an effective or even efficient public relations campaign.*

HOW FAR AFIELD YOU'VE DISSEMINATED YOUR MESSAGE(S): Again, this is easy to track. How many media outlets received and used your news releases? How many electronic newsletters did you distribute? Where were they sent? Whereas this may seem like a step forward from simply counting your productivity, again it lacks validity since it does not measure communication effects, unless, of course, publicity is all you are looking for. The extent to which your message is exposed to people in general is an outdated way of looking at the effects of the public relations effort even if the channels are online. Media monitoring seems to be one of the most widely used tracking methods for public relations departments, but again it lacks validity in terms of relationship outcomes with one possible exception. If you are working toward enhancing your organization's reputation with the media, you might be concerned that they begin to actually use your material. Keep in mind, however, that extrapolating to how many members of other publics saw and understood your message is dangerously lacking in substance. But there are also other reasons for doing media monitoring on a regular basis. We'll examine these later.

THE ACCURACY OF YOUR MESSAGE: Now we're beginning to look more at the qualitative aspect of the outcomes, rather than simply the quantitative aspects of the work that's been done. Assessing message accuracy in this way usually refers to the use of uncontrolled media. In other words, when you are using controlled media, the accuracy of the message is controlled by you at an earlier stage in the public relations process. On the other hand, the accuracy of the messages disseminated through mass media, for example, cannot be measured until it's really too late to do much about it. Thus, media monitoring that includes content analysis is useful and essential to an ongoing evaluation. Simply measuring the extent to which they "got it right" though, is again not a real communication effect, but a process effect.

WHETHER OR NOT ANYONE IN YOUR TARGET PUBLIC SAW OR HEARD THE MESSAGE THAT YOU ACTUALLY SENT: This can be a useful way to evaluate the appropriateness of your selected channels and vehicles. It is necessary to find a way to ask members of your specific target public if they heard or saw your messages, and if they heard or saw them accurately. Even if you count "clicks" or "likes" you have no way of knowing if the publics who responded in this way actually understood your message or substantively acted upon it. This is not a response that provides you with constructive information.

CHANGE IN KNOWLEDGE LEVEL OF YOUR TARGET PUBLIC: They say that knowledge is power and so it would seem that developing a communication program to enhance a public's knowledge level about your organization or issue is a powerful communication outcome. It can be, but it isn't necessarily. Clearly, an enhancement of a public's knowledge as a result of successful message dissemination is a positive outcome. Before we consider why it might not be the appropriate ultimate outcome that you need to measure the success or failure of your campaign, let's consider a public information campaign where the communication outcome that you want to achieve is, indeed, an increase in knowledge level.

In assessing the outcome of a public information campaign, whether it focuses on the prevention of skin cancer or on the nutritional aspects of dairy products, measurement of knowledge level is a valid way to evaluate the degree of success. How you carry out that evaluation accurately, however, is a complex issue. First, it's necessary to have an accurate picture of your target public's level of knowledge about the subject before the communication campaign begins. This may require what researchers call a *pre-test–post-test design*. This technique involves assessing knowledge level before the application of the messages, and then after the campaign is complete to make comparisons. To do this accurately involves the use of scientifically designed surveys, which requires a high level of knowledge about research methods and can be expensive.

It's important to point out that whereas knowledge may be a substantial first step in the development of sound relationships with your organization's publics, it's highly likely that even this kind of accurate measurement of knowledge outcomes doesn't really get to the heart of what you want to achieve. To do that you need to consider the attitude, behavior, and relationship changes that you're really looking for.

CHANGE IN ATTITUDE AND BEHAVIOR OF YOUR TARGET PUBLIC: The most powerful changes a public relations campaign can facilitate in a target public are changes in attitude (which can lead to expression of those changed attitudes or what we know as public opinion), and behavior. Consider a communication campaign about the hazards of binge drinking targeted at university-aged students. If the only communication outcome from the campaign is an increase in the students' knowledge level about binge drinking and its long-term health effects, then the campaign is really only partially effective. What such a campaign really should be looking for is changes in attitude that have the potential to change their personal behavior and that might lead to a decrease in the number of times they put themselves at risk. In this kind of situation, however, the only way to accurately measure a change in behavior is to ask.

There are other instances in public relations where the change in behavior might be measured more objectively. You may design a plan to support sales; in this case increased consumer spending on particular items would be useful behavioral measures. A plan designed to recruit volunteers would count the actual numbers of volunteers. A plan to support corporate sponsorship would measure financial gains in sponsorship. The advantage of behavior measurement is that it is concrete and thus a valid measure of public relations outcomes. The problem is that the actual issue may be more esoteric.

For example, if the plan focuses on employee relations and deals with a problem of employees not seeming to respect and support one another, you may have to be more creative to find a way to measure an improvement in respect. You can hardly measure the amount of respect. But you might be able to keep track of employee involvement in a particular project that requires them to utilize one another's skills. As the public relations practitioner, it's your job to design that project.

CHANGE IN QUALITY OF THE RELATIONSHIP: This is at the heart of public relations and warrants its own discussion in the next section.

EVALUATING RELATIONSHIPS

At the heart of public relations is the focus on the development and maintenance of mutually beneficial relationships between organizations and their important publics. Although the foregoing discussion of the communication outcomes we can reasonably measure is useful in the measurement of direct communication outcomes, there is more to evaluation. The problem is: how do you measure something that is as seemingly intangible as a "relationship" between two entities?

There is no doubt that measuring relationships is difficult; however, it is still a very important component of determining the effectiveness of public relations outcomes. Back in 1999, two highly-regarded public relations scholars James Grunig and Linda Childers Hon published one of the first papers exploring just how this could be done. In that paper, published by the Institute for Public Relations (see reference in Chapter 6: A Resource List for PR Managers) they identified a number of elements that might constitute the expected outcomes of a successful project or campaign designed to develop, enhance, or maintain relationships with important publics. These elements are as follows:

1. **CONTROL MUTUALITY**: This element describes the way in which the organization and its public(s) view the amount of influence one has on the other. For example, if an important public perceives that a particular organization exerts too much power over them, this creates a significant imbalance that will have an impact on how that public interacts with the organization.

2. **TRUST**: Trust is a significant aspect of any relationship, whether it is between two individuals, a professor and student, or an organization and its publics. From a public relations perspective, in determining the health of a relationship between an organization and an important public, it measures the extent to which a public has confidence that the organization will do as it says.

3. **SATISFACTION**: A key element of any transactional relationship (including marketing), satisfaction measures quantify how happy the public is with the organization. The extent to which, as Grunig and Childers say: ". . . the benefits outweigh the costs. . ." of maintaining that relationship (see p. 20 of the IPR paper).

4. **COMMITMENT**: Just as in interpersonal relationships, commitment means that the public believes the relationship is worth the effort of maintaining it.

But remember, this goes both ways. An organization needs to consider how committed it is to maintaining a relationship with any identified public before embarking on a PR plan.

Although these elements of relationships were identified some years ago, they continue to represent the most salient features that lend themselves to measurement of one sort or another. The problem is that they can be a bit insubstantial and are often measured based on data about perceptions. Asking members of an important public "How do you feel?" about the organization is one way to elicit such information, but is often not considered hard data. So you have to explore other ways of getting to the information you need.

Marketers, for example, might use repeat sales figures to measure commitment. PR practitioners might use percentage of positive Facebook comments as a measure of satisfaction. These measures are more concrete.

In Chapter 3, in our discussion of the planning phase of the public relations process, we considered the issue of *relationship objectives*. If you have developed specific objectives related to the degree of trust that the publics have for the organization, the extent to which they feel positively disposed toward the organization's products/services, policies and activities, and the extent to which the publics feel that the organization gives back to them, then you also need to determine a way to measure these aspects of the relationship.

Some concrete examples of methods that you might use to gather data about the quality of the relationship include the following:

- opinion surveys conducted by the organization

- opinion surveys conducted by independent third parties

- opinion surveys both before and after a campaign or project (this is a pre-test–post-test design for evaluation research)

- focus groups

- hotline feedback

- community participation in organizational events

- media monitoring (limited and indirect, but useful)

- measures of social media engagement.

What is important in the application of any of these evaluation strategies is the quality and content of the questions posed in the instruments. You can refer to the more in-depth materials suggested in the resource chapter for suggestions about the development of these materials.

In the end, the relationships that an organization has with its important publics are reflected in its reputation, and reputation is really nothing more than public perception of the organization. Reputation, however, is a key asset to the ability of any organization—whether the organization is not-for-profit, profit making, or government—to flourish. Thus, considering the impacts on relationships of any public relations activities is at the heart of evaluation.

MEASURING SOCIAL MEDIA OUTCOMES

As we have discussed throughout this book, the advent of social media has changed forever the practice of public relations. Thus, in spite of the fact that social media does not and should not stand alone as your only public relations and communication tools, it is important enough to consider its measurement in its own category. The fundamental bottom line on measuring social media is not in figuring out how many people "like" you on Facebook, follow you on Instagram or retweet your *bon mots*; rather the key is to determine the value of this social media effort to the achievement of communication and public relations objectives and in turn organizational goals. That being said, as you explore how social media is generally measured, and identify tools available for this measurement, you'll quickly figure out that the following three metrics that are widely used begin to capture a picture of the extent to which an organization's social media efforts contribute to the bottom line. You'll also notice that they are largely quantitative and do not begin to paint a picture of the qualitative nature of your relationships with your public:

1. **EXPOSURE**: The number of people reached with specific messages.

2. **ENGAGEMENT**: The number of the people exposed to your messages who actually acted on the specific messages.

3. **INFLUENCE**: The number of people who acted on your specific messages who then used their own online presence to expose your message to even more people.

4. **SHARE OF VOICE**: The percentage of relevant conversations that are about your organization/brand/message versus your competitors.

The validity of each of these social media impacts as a measurement of the success of a particular campaign is related to the objectives that were developed at the outset of a project or campaign. As with any communication tool or tactic implemented,

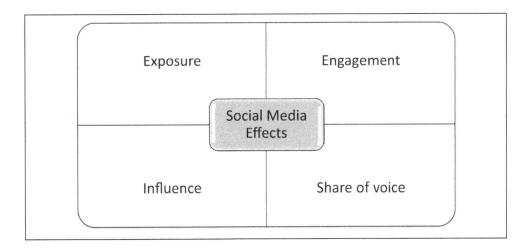

FIGURE 5.3 The Social Media Metrics Matrix

those measurable outcome objectives we discussed in Chapter 3 actually have imbedded in them the metrics you should be examining. However, if those outcome objectives are not valid, your measurement will not be either. You need to keep this in mind as you embark upon selecting from among the plethora of available tools for measuring social media impacts.

THE "BENCHMARK"

Before we complete our discussion of evaluation, there is one more evaluation-related business concept that is worth discussing. That is the issue of *benchmarking*. Depending on where you do your reading about benchmarking, you may find one of several different takes on a definition:

> A BENCHMARK is a standard against which you
> may compare or judge something.

Some people use the word to refer to the practice of seeking out how the successful competition does what they do, and setting that up as the standard against which your organization can compare itself. In the field of public relations, this kind of a benchmark is very difficult to obtain and not especially useful. This is at least partly a result of the fact that much of what public relations accomplishes seems intangible (a good argument for making your evaluation plan as tangible as possible). And it is partly because public relations objectives and results are organization-specific.

Another way of looking at benchmarking is somewhat more useful in the evaluation of the public relations effort. This involves using your own public relations efforts of the past as standards against which you'll measure the outcomes of the future. Clearly, this involves the ongoing collection of data for comparison, and regular auditing of the ongoing public relations program, in addition to the more short-term campaigns.

In any case, the contribution that public relations projects make to the bottom line of any organization must be evaluated on a regular basis.

USING THE WORKSHEETS

The final two worksheets included here include a **MEDIA MONITORING TRACKING SHEET** and a **CHECKLIST FOR ONGOING SOCIAL MEDIA TRACKING**.

Every organization that does media monitoring has its own version of a media monitoring form. It is included here not because it's the most reliable way to measure the success of public relations (far from it, as we have already discussed), but it is an activity that most organizations ought to be doing on a regular basis. This traditional approach to media monitoring can be applied to online media as well as the more traditional outlets. However, you will need a different approach to monitor actual social media.

The second worksheet provides you with a checklist to consider ongoing social media engagement. The resources provided in Chapter 6 will provide you with further ideas as to how you might expand this.

Media Monitoring Tracking Sheet

Use this sheet for on-going or project-specific monitoring of traditional and online media.

Date	Media Source[1]	Direction[2]	Description[3]	Origination[4]	Evaluation & Follow-up

[1] Television, radio, print paper, magazine, online news source, blog
[2] Positive, negative, neutral
[3] Story type (news, feature etc.), byline, summary
[4] Outgoing media release, outgoing query/pitch, incoming query/pitch, outside the organization

Checklist for On-going Social Media Tracking

Flesh out this checklist to reflect your organization or project-specific social media plan schedule.

☐ Respond to inbound social media messages daily

☐ Monitor brand mentions daily

☐ Respond to brand mentions daily

☐ Monitor for keywords daily

☐ Monitor the competition daily

☐ Prepare relevant content weekly

☐ Post to relevant social media accounts as per prescribed schedule
- o Facebook
- o Twitter
- o Instagram
- o LinkedIn
- o YouTube
- o Other _____

CHAPTER 6

A Resource List for PR Managers

This chapter provides you with a variety of resources that you will find helpful as you gain expertise in the development of strategic, ethical public relations and communications plans. They are organized by topics that reflect the foregoing chapters.

On its own, this workbook does not pretend to provide the background theory and practice base that a professional public relations practitioner ought to have to provide clients and employers with optimal public relations programming. If, however, you wish to enhance your skills, the resources presented here will help you to think a bit more critically about what you do and what you see other public relations managers doing with their projects.

It is also important to remember that there is more than one way to interpret and apply the public relations process. Consulting a variety of academic and industry resources will allow you to see different ways of viewing the same process.

CHAPTER 1: PR PROJECT PLANNING IN THE TWENTY-FIRST CENTURY

The readings and web resources selected to enhance the introductory chapter include a range of well-known, general textbooks in public relations as well as selected articles from both trade publications, academic journals, and websites on the general subject of what constitutes public relations practice in the twenty-first century and on ethics as an integral part of the PR planning process. The textbooks also include varying approaches to the four-step public relations process. The older resources included in this list are now considered to be classics.

Foundational Textbooks

Broom, G. & Sha, B. (2012). *Cutlip & Center's Effective Public Relations*. 11th ed. Harlow, UK: Pearson.

Richardson, K. & Hinton, M. (2015). *Applied Public Relations: Cases in Stakeholder Management*. 3rd ed. Abingdon, UK: Routledge.

Seitel, F. (2016). *The Practice of Public Relations*. 16th ed. Harlow, UK: Pearson.

Planning Textbooks

Austin, E.A. & Pinkleton, B. (2015). *Strategic Public Relations Management: Planning and Managing Effective Public Relations Campaigns*. 3rd ed. Abingdon, UK: Routledge.

Smith, R. (2017). *Strategic Planning for Public Relations*. 5th ed. Abingdon, UK: Routledge.

Ethics Textbooks

Martin, D. & Wright, D. (2015). *Public Relations Ethics: How to Practice PR without Losing your Soul*. New York: Business Expert Press.

Parsons, P. (2016). *Ethics in Public Relations: A Guide to Best Practice*. London: Kogan Page.

Articles

Barnett, N. (2007). The PR Response to Virginia Tech and Beyond. *Communication World*, 24(4), 14–15.

Burnette-Lemon, J. (2017). The Perks and Pitfalls of Strategic Communication Planning: A Q&A with Caroline Kealey. *Communication World*, 1 February 2017, 1–3.

Web Resources

Canadian Public Relations Society. CPRS Public Relations Definition. www.cprs.ca/aboutus/mission.aspx

Cision. (2014). Six Ways Social Media has Changed PR. www.cision.com/us/2014/09/6-ways-social-media-changed-public-relations/

Chartered Institute of Public Relations. CIPR Definition of Public Relations. www.cipr.co.uk/content/careers-advice/what-pr

Public Relations Society of America. General Information on the Practice of Public Relations (PRSA). www.prsa.org/about/about-pr/all-about-pr/

Whitely, M. (2013). Strategic Public Relations Planning: Positioning for Success. *PRSay*: PRSA blog, 27 August 2013. https://prsay.prsa.org/2013/08/27/strategic-public-relations-planning-positioning-for-success/

Wynne, R. (2015). Five Ways the Internet Hasn't Changed PR. *Forbes*, 28 April 2015. www.forbes.com/sites/robertwynne/2015/04/28/five-ways-the-internet-hasnt-changed-public-relations/#17af3b0b1305

CHAPTER 2: THE RESEARCH PHASE

The following resources provide both food for thought about how research fits into the public relations process, as well as further detailed information how to conduct this research. Anyone who will be engaged in carrying out in-depth research, especially formalized processes such as surveys or focus groups, needs further study to develop knowledge and skills. In addition, researchers need a much more focused knowledge in statistical procedures.

Textbooks

Gregory, A. (2015). *Planning and Managing Public Relations Campaigns: A Strategic Approach*. 4th ed. London: Kogan-Page.

Stacks, D. (2016). *Primer of Public Relations Research*. 3rd ed. New York: The Guilford Press.

Articles

Clary, S. (2008). You Are What You Know: Research for Campaign Success. *PR Tactics*, 15(1), 10.

Gregory, A. & Watson, T. (2008). Defining the Gap Between Research and Practice in Public Relations Programme Evaluation—Towards a New Research Agenda. *Journal of Marketing Communications*, 14(5), 337–350. doi:10.1080/13527260701869098

Web Resources

Parsons, P. (2015). Academic Research in Public Relations: Making it Useful to Practitioners. https://professorparsons.com/2015/10/06/academic-research-in-public-relations-making-it-useful-to-practitioners/

Pew Research Center. (2016). Social Media Update 2016: Facebook Usage and Engagement is on the Rise, While Adoption of Other Platforms Holds Steady. 11 November 2016. www.pewinternet.org/2016/11/11/social-media-update-2016/

Public Relations Society of America. Measurement Resources. https://apps.prsa.org/Intelligence/BusinessCase/MeasurementResources/#.WOOsvOT2Z9A

Public Relations Society of America. (2014). How to Conduct an Effective Social Media Audit. 2 October 2014. http://prsay.prsa.org/2014/10/02/how-to-conduct-an-effective-social-media-audit/

Williams, S. (2013). Is That All There Is? A Literature Review and Potential Approach to Measuring Influence in Social Media. 10 April 2013. www.instituteforpr.org/topics/is-that-all-there-is-a-literature-review-and-potential-approach-to-measuring-influence-in-social-media/

CHAPTER 3: THE PLANNING PHASE

You can find important information on the planning phase of the public relations process in the foundational textbooks suggested under Chapter 1 resources. The following resources are provided for you to gain additional information and different approaches to the planning phase.

Articles

Holtz, S. (2013). Socially Relevant. *Communication World*, 30(2), 8–11.

Kuenn, A. (2013). 6 Tips for Crafting a Social Media Content Strategy. *Communication World*, 30(3), 9–10.

Pophal, L. (2014). How to Sell Social Media to the C-Suite. *Communication World*, 31(2), 22–25.

Web Resources

Aanenson, A. (2014). Avoiding PR disasters: Five tips for integrating social media into your communication plan. *Forbes*, 23 April 2013. www.forbes.com/sites/sungardas/2014/04/23/avoiding-pr-disasters-5-tips-for-integrating-social-media-into-your-communication-plans/

Anonymous. (2014). Not Every PR Plan Needs Social Media. *The Guardian* online, 21 November 2014. www.theguardian.com/media-network/2014/nov/21/social-media-pr-plan-communication

Odden, L. Integrating public relations and content marketing: It doesn't have to be scary. *Top Rank Blog*. www.toprankblog.com/2013/10/integrating-public-relations-content-marketing/

Taylor, H. & Goeres, K. The Basics of Integrating Social Media into your PR Plan. www.slideshare.net/MyCorporation/mbawi-620-basics-of-integrating-social-media-into-your-pr-plan

CHAPTER 4: MANAGING IMPLEMENTATION

There is a wealth of information written about management in general. To find out more about the history of management and general management principles, any good management textbook aimed at a broad business audience will be useful. The following materials are selected to focus you in the direction of managing public relations projects.

Web Resources

Henry, A. (2013). Five Best Personal Project Management Tools. *LifeHacker*, 6 October 2013. http://lifehacker.com/five-best-personal-project-management-tools-1441334694

Mochal, T. (2009). 10 Best Practices for Successful Project Management. *TechRepublic*, 23 July 2009. www.techrepublic.com/blog/10-things/10-best-practices-for-successful-project-management/

Nazar, J. (2013). 30 Terrific Tools for Small Businesses. *Forbes*, 28 May 2013. www.forbes.com/sites/jasonnazar/2013/05/28/30-terrific-tools-for-small-businesses/

Schiff, J. (2012). 12 Common Project Management Mistakes—and How to Avoid Them. *CIO*, 26 September 2012. www.cio.com/article/2391872/project-manage ment/12-common-project-management-mistakes--and-how-to-avoid-them.html

CHAPTER 5: THE EVALUATION PHASE

Just as for the Chapter 4 resources previously, you may want to read about evaluation in the general management literature, but here are some selected resources about evaluation in public relations. Some of these will give you more detailed information about the "how-to" of some evaluation tools.

Textbooks

Flesch, R. (1951). *How to Test Readability*. New York: Harper & Row. (A classic text.)

Li, C. & Stacks, D. (2015). *Measuring the Impact of Social Media on Business Profit & Success*. New York: Peter Lang.

Paine, K. (2011). *Measure What Matters: Online Tools for Understanding Customers, Social Media, Engagement and Key Relationships*. New York: Wiley.

Watson, T. & Noble, P. (2014). *Evaluating Public Relations: A Guide to Planning, Research and Measurement*. London: Kogan-Page.

Web Resources

Adweek. (2016). Updated Checklist for Social Media Managers. 14 March 2016. www.adweek.com/digital/sprout-social-michael-patterson-updated-checklist-for-social-media-managers-infographic/

Agius, A. (2016). 10 Metrics to Track for Social Media Success. *Social Media Examiner*, 8 November 2016. www.socialmediaexaminer.com/10-metrics-to-track-for-social-media-success/

AMEC. (2015). Barcelona Principles: The Development and the Detailed Changes. http://amecorg.com/wp-content/uploads/2015/09/Barcelona-Principles-2.0-develop ment-and-detailed-changes.-7-September-2015.pdf

Buffer blog. (2015). Social Media Checklist: Daily, Weekly, Monthly (downloadable pdf). 27 August 2015. https://bufferblog-wpengine.netdna-ssl.com/wp-content/uploads/2015/08/Daily-Social-Media-Checklist.pdf

Grunig, J. & Hon, L. (2011). Guidelines for Measuring Relationships in Public Relations. *Institute for Public Relations*, 16 June 2011. www.instituteforpr.org/measuring-relationships/

Jeffrey, A. (2013). Social Media Measurement: A Step-by-Step Approach. *Institute for Public Relations*, 6 June 2013. www.instituteforpr.org/social-media-measurement-a-step-by-step-approach/

Public Relations Plan: Sample Format

Public Relations Plan

SAMPLE FORMAT

Prepared for:

CLIENT NAME

Date

Prepared by: Team Names
COMPANY NAME | COMPANY ADDRESS

CONTENTS

PURPOSE STATEMENT

State the purpose of this document and who prepared it. This is also the place to explain the public relations terminology that you may be using throughout the plan. Not every client/employer will understand even the PR meaning of the term "publics," for example.

This purpose statement should be on a page by itself.

EXECUTIVE SUMMARY

Give a brief, concise summary of the strategy that follows.

Summarize the public relations problem(s) or opportunity(ies), delineate the overall goal of the plan, summarize the specific objectives, delineate key publics and why you have selected the priorities. Summarize the messages and highlight the key communications vehicles recommended in the plan. Finally, summarize how and why this plan will be evaluated. If you think it would be helpful, subheadings may be used in the executive summary.

This is a summary, not an introduction. It should be limited to two pages. It should begin on its own page and when the summary is complete, begin the body of the plan on a new page. Remember that this is a business document. It should be written in a business-oriented voice: it is neither an academic paper nor a letter to a friend.

ORGANIZATIONAL BACKGROUND

In this section you'll give an overview of the client. Provide basic information about the organization's name and location in this introduction. Describe the nature of the business and what kind of business it is (partnership, private, public, whatever).

You may wonder why it is necessary to provide this kind of information to the client who presumably already knows more about the organization than you do. It has two main purposes: it assures the client that you are accurately informed about the organization, and it also puts the information in a new framework for the client to see that you are viewing it in a specific way.

HISTORY, MISSION, AND STRUCTURE

Begin with a statement about the origins of the organization. Then provide the mission statement and reference to any other important guiding principles that help to understand the function and direction of the organization. The organizational chart and a brief narrative explanation of it should also be included so that internal relationships may be delineated.

The structure and function of the public relations/communication role in the organization should also be presented here.

ENVIRONMENTAL PRESSURES

This section provides a narrative description of the external environment within which the organization functions. It places the organization in the context of its overall industry and discusses the political, social, economic and technological pressures that play a part in the function of both the industry in general and this organization in particular.

After the narrative description, the pressures are summarized in a list.

PUBLIC RELATIONS/COMMUNICATIONS ANALYSIS

INTRODUCTION TO THE ANALYSIS

This introduction explains how the data were collected and what sources were used in the ensuing analysis of communications / public relations issues. If this is a very large plan, a list of interviewees as well as the instruments used to collect data should be included in the appendix. In addition, a data analysis table may be included in the appendix.

Also included here are explanations of any limitations or delimitations on the data collection process and the time frame during which the analysis occurred.

INTERNAL PUBLICS

This section begins with an explanation of the importance of internal constituencies to this particular organization. This introduction is followed by a description of each important internal public identified during the data collection and a description of that public's relationship with the organization. This is not merely a listing, but a detailed description of the public. Subheadings are used to identify each public.

EXTERNAL PUBLICS

This section is similar to the foregoing, but focuses on external publics– their characteristics and their relationship with the focal organization. These two groupings of publics are generic and somewhat arbitrary. Under certain circumstances, the publics should be categorized differently. For example, when creating a plan to address a controversial issue, rather than dividing the publics generally into internal and external groups, the broad groupings would include proponents, opponents, and neutral publics.

IDENTIFICATION OF PRIORITY PUBLICS

After the data have been explained in the descriptions of the publics, this section begins the analysis. The reason for selection of the priorities is provided and then the priority publics that will be addressed in this strategic plan are identified in rank order. If this is a multiyear plan, priorities for each year are identified.

EMERGING ISSUES

Part of the analysis involves addressing the public relations and communications issues, both internal and external, that are emerging, but may not yet be affecting the organization.

STRENGTHS AND WEAKNESSES

This is the narrative description of the data table that you may include in the appendix. It analyzes the current state of the communications and relationships between the organization and its currently identified publics. It also takes into consideration the current situation regarding the public relations management within the organization concluding with a list of strengths and a list of weaknesses in communications and relationships.

PUBLIC RELATIONS PROBLEMS AND OPPORTUNITIES

From the strengths and weaknesses previously identified some problems and opportunities become evident. Strengths generally give rise to opportunities upon which the organization can capitalize, whereas weaknesses help to identify problems that require solutions. The narrative description is followed by a list of strengths and weaknesses. A priority problem/opportunity may also be identified.

PUBLICS, OBJECTIVES AND MESSAGES

THE STRATEGIC GOAL

The strategic goal is a specific statement of the overall goal that this strategic public relations plan will address. Specifying this relies on the accurate identification of problems and opportunities.

OUTCOME OBJECTIVES

Strategic objectives are those outcomes toward which this plan will strive for each priority public. Because some of the objectives will overlap one or more publics, these outcome objectives may either be provided for each individual public or for specific groupings. For example, the outcome objectives may be the same for all internal publics.

CORE MESSAGE

It is very important to be specific and to provide a succinct statement that encapsulates the overall strategic message. This message should underlie any messages that are communicated by both word and deed in the strategy to achieve the strategic goal.

It may also be necessary to break down the message to be more audience-specific by reworking it for specific publics. These more targeted messages are also presented in this section.

STRATEGIC APPROACHES

This section describes exactly what approaches the organization will take to meet the specific objectives set out previously for each public.

There are various approaches to presenting these. However, linking these strategies to the objectives they are designed to achieve is key.

STRATEGIES AND RATIONALES

Not only are the strategies described (e.g. an event, print publication(s), the development of an award, a community activity, new media policies, media training for executives, a web-based strategy, implementation of a hotline etc.), but rationales are provided. Why was this approach selected? How do we know that it is likely to have the desired effects?

These proposed approaches are described in as much detail as possible. The following questions should be answered:

- What is planned?
- When will the development take place?
- When will it be completed?
- Who will do what parts of it?
- How much will it cost in terms of resources and money?
- What will it look like?
- Why are you proposing this strategy?

TIMELINE FOR IMPLEMENTATION

This is a summary of the individual time considerations presented in the previous section. Some kind of time management tool may be included in the appendix.

THE BUDGET

Summarize the budget in this section using a narrative approach. A detailed budget table or spread sheet should be included in the appendix of the plan.

EVALUATION STRATEGIES

EVALUATION APPROACHES AND RATIONALES

Each strategy proposed in the previous section needs to be evaluated in terms of the objectives it was designed to achieve.

This section answers the question: How will we know if the strategy was successful and how will we measure it? It also addresses the issue of why a particular evaluation strategy is proposed.

If data collection is indicated (such as media monitoring), the plan needs to provide an instrument for this purpose. The instrument itself is placed in the appendix.

APPENDICES TO THE PLAN

Samples of inclusions in the appendices:

- Data sources for the analysis (list of who was interviewed, etc.)
- Interview guidelines
- Data table
- Resources required for implementation
- Budget
- Time management materials (e.g. a Gantt chart)
- Samples of evaluation tools
- Sample template for web sites or any other tools proposed